ONE STEP
CLOSER

This book is presented on behalf
of the Elmer N. Witt Initiative
for Creative Leadership, an
endowment supported by family
and friends to advance leadership in youth and
young adult ministry. Elmer served in campus
ministry at Governors State University and as
Regional Director from 1972 to 1983.

Celebrate

LUTHERAN **C** 1907

CAMPUS MINISTRY

2007   Expanding Minds
Deepening Faith
Inspiring Service

EVANGELICAL LUTHERAN CHURCH IN AMERICA

ONE STEP CLOSER

WHY U2 MATTERS TO THOSE SEEKING GOD

CHRISTIAN SCHAREN

Brazos Press
Grand Rapids, Michigan

© 2006 by Christian Scharen

Published by Brazos Press
a division of Baker Publishing Group
P.O. Box 6287, Grand Rapids, MI 49516-6287
www.brazospress.com

Second printing, March 2006

Printed in the United States of America

Library of Congress Cataloging-in-Publication Data
Scharen, Christian Batalden.
  One step closer : why U2 matters to those seeking God / Christian Scharen.
      p.   cm.
    Includes bibliographical references.
    ISBN 10: 1-58743-169-6 (pbk.)
    ISBN 978-1-58743-169-2 (pbk.)
      1. U2 (Musical group) 2. Rock music—Religious aspects—Christianity.
  3. Rock musicians—Ireland—Biography. I. Title.
  ML421.U2S33 2006
  782.42166092′2—dc22   2005028470

To Isaiah and Grace, beloved children,
And to Rose Delesani,
their sponsor-sister in Milambe, Malawi
(For more on sponsorship,
see www.savethechildren.org)

CONTENTS

INTRODUCTION

One Step Closer . . .

There's cathedrals and the alleyways in our music. I think the alleyway is usually on the way to the cathedral, where you can hear your own footsteps and you're slightly nervous and looking over your shoulder and wondering if there's somebody following you. And then you get there and you realize there was somebody following you: it's God.

Bono

A Wide Tradition

I hope that you've found this book because you, too, find yourself drawn into the ways Bono and U2 talk of spiritual matters. I've been a fan since I first heard them in 1985. I've always felt a spiritual kinship with them, as though they seem to know my soul and put words to thoughts I've had. They've been spiritual companions for me. This is true during times when I've felt at home in a traditional church, but even more

9

so during times when I've felt frustrated with the church. When my life is in spiritual upheaval, U2 has been and is a trustworthy companion. For a long while I appreciated this, as one appreciates a cool uncle or a favorite aunt. Only recently when a group of college students asked me to lead a retreat for them did I begin to think about revisiting U2 in an effort to think through their spiritual voice in a more organized way.

I don't mean to be scolding in this effort to think through U2's spiritual voice as so many Christians have done when they've questioned if U2's members and music are sufficiently "Christian." That question is humorous if you reflect on the ways U2 has turned the question back on the church, asking whether the church is sufficiently Christian! Rather, what I mean to do here is to think about how U2 fits within a longer tradition of Christian voices that point us to the cross, to Jesus, and to the power of God's ways in the world. By seeing them in a fuller light, I'm trying to make some sense of how they fit into a certain tradition of speaking and living faith. It is worth doing because many preachers "preach to the choir," so to speak, while U2 "preaches" to millions who don't even know the basic songs of faith and have grown up without any connection to the church.

When I think of preachers who reach millions, I usually think of Billy Graham, Rick Warren, or others like them who speak to thousands with Christ's message. U2's "preaching" is strikingly different from the stereotypical television preacher (the kind Bono criticized in songs and finally lampooned in his Mirror Ball Man persona during the 1990s). I want to say to all the fans of U2 who don't go to church, who don't know that the Christian tradition is a wide and generous place with room for many voices: listen! The voice of U2 is not unique; it is deeply rooted in authentic Christianity. I want to invite you into that generous and wide tradition and introduce you to

10

some of those saints and friends of God who have also spoken as U2 does about faith in the midst of doubt, hope in the face of despair, love in the face of violence, and peace and justice in the face of suffering.

This book is not about the meaning of U2 songs nor is it a chronicling of their spiritual journey from *Boy* to *How to Dismantle an Atomic Bomb*. It is not an investigation of the private life of Bono or any one member of the band. Neither is it intended first of all for those within the church as an effort either to defend U2's faith or to explain the usefulness of their lyrics for preaching to spiritually hungry but religiously disaffected young people.

Theology in a Minor Key

This book is an attempt to reveal to those unfamiliar with Christianity that the Christian tradition has, metaphorically speaking, many "keys." Some of Christianity's most prominent voices play major keys, claiming for instance that God has laid a special blessing on the United States or that God will lay a special blessing on you if you write out your check to this or to that church or ministry. Others claim that if you come to church, you will find everything to your liking, from the cookies and coffee to the pop music and practical, uplifting messages. Rather than speak in these major keys, this book introduces you to a minor key—what I call the theology of the cross—that fits U2's voice. I will expand on this later in the book, but let me give a quick introduction to that perspective here.

The theology of the cross fits U2 because it avoids the all too common proclamation of faith, hope, and love that ignores the present realities of doubt, despair, suffering, and injustice. It is a tradition that looks at the world and speaks the truth about what it sees: the good, the bad, and the ugly. In the words of the church reformer Martin Luther, the theology of the cross "calls a thing what it really is." The honesty of this theological voice is freeing because it faces up to our experiences of the truth of life. One need not ignore or be surprised by the many difficulties and sorrows in life. Rather, such faith allows us to take life's challenges straight on knowing that in our struggles we are not alone. Jesus, the crucified and risen one, has already faced the worst of life.

This book, therefore, will help you make sense of U2's style of talking about God, Jesus, the Spirit, and the Christian life in a holistic way, rooted deeply in the history of faith we who follow Jesus share. As I will talk about more in the last chapter, it is a way of speaking (or singing!) the truth, but even more than that, it is a way of living the truth. Now I'll briefly tell a little about my spiritual journey and how I found U2 along the way.

Closer to . . . What?

I thought I'd already found Jesus. I'm thinking of a time during my first years at university. My childhood friend, Nick, had gone to a Christian college in Seattle, Washington, while I attended a Christian college in Tacoma, just a few miles south along the Puget Sound. During high school in Montana, Nick had been the good boy. He was on the varsity basketball team, and he was an academic merit scholar and a nice guy whose family went to a church where they praised the Lord. I was an average football player, a below-average student, I was on the edge of trouble, and to top it off, I'd dropped out of church after ninth grade when our family's church had an ugly split over a pastor. A group in the congregation didn't like this pastor and so withheld their pledges of financial support to force him out. He left, we left, and I left. If that was Christian community, I could do without it.

I arrived at college with an individual spirituality I'd found through imagining my own success. Jesus was my friend and wanted me to succeed. My version of the gospel was rooted in a few verses taken out of context, such as "ask and it will be given to you" (Matthew 7:7, NIV) and "all things are possible with God" (Mark 10:27, NIV). I went to a Christian college because of their football team, still hoping I was better than I really was. Such an attitude fit my faith at the time, too. I went to different churches with friends, hoping my faith was better than it really was. I had no sense of purpose, and although I seemed successful from the outside, I was caving in. It turns out that my years away from church had helped me find a spirituality that was too thin, too small, too shallow. My personal faith that Jesus would help me succeed wasn't deep enough to create any real change in me, especially when I felt I was failing.

During these first years at college, I'd sometimes go up to visit my friend Nick in Seattle. I looked to him for support since he was the one who had the solid faith and credentials for college success. He'd done the right things in high school, and he was positioned to do really well in college and in life. Usually, I'd just go for the day and we'd hang out or go to the mall or go to lunch at Pike's Place Market, a downtown outdoor gathering place. One of the last times I saw him, however, was in the winter of our sophomore year when I spent the weekend with him. Two things happened that weekend that had an impact on my life.

The first event was about music. I'd grown up on rock music—from classics like the Rolling Stones, the Beatles, and the Who to 1980s groups like the Clash, REM, and the Talking Heads. On that weekend, Nick's roommate played the first

"Christian" rock music I'd ever heard. It was by a band called U2, and I made copies of all his cassettes. I was captivated by the pulsing and God-haunted sounds of "October," "Sunday Bloody Sunday," "Gloria," and "I Will Follow." As I listened, something clicked together that had never before met: my faith and what you might describe as my culture — the music, friends, and life I lived from day to day.

The second event was about drugs. I'd grown up in small-town America, so drinking a beer was no surprise to me. During high school, we used to sneak into the fraternity parties at the college in the town where I grew up. But Seattle is not small-town America. Nick took me to a party at the University of Washington where people were smoking marijuana and other things I didn't recognize — the first time I'd seen drugs like this. I remember being totally shocked while wanting to seem totally cool. But truthfully, having come from listening to U2 in Nick's apartment to now seeing people making bongs out of cola cans and sniffing powder up their noses like I'd only seen in movies was too much. I had been drinking, but all of a sudden I experienced a sobering surge of fear and heard voices exploding in my head saying "get out."

After that weekend, I went home feeling sad and confused. Who was I, and who was my friend I thought I knew? What were we supposed to be and do? What mattered? I teetered on the verge of personal collapse. After throwing myself into training for football and failing to get the preseason invitation that all varsity players receive, I faced the fact that I was pouring my energy into the wrong place. I quit football. I floated, not knowing what to do or where to turn. Jesus had not worked it out for me. I thought I'd found Jesus and that he was my man, the one to help me succeed. And when I failed, I felt I'd lost him.

14

In the midst of these struggles Jesus found me and turned my life upside down. I began attending the campus church on Sundays. A new team of campus pastors had begun in my second year, and they genuinely seemed to make space for questions. I wasn't ready to toss out my faith yet. One night that fall, a religion professor was presenting a lecture on homelessness in the Seattle-Tacoma area. I went not knowing what to expect. There I learned that four thousand people slept on the streets each night, and many more were hungry and had inadequate housing. As if for the first time, I stopped looking in the mirror, and I looked at the world. I saw tremendous, shocking, and inexcusable suffering. I vowed that night that I would work to change this. I call it my conversion experience—the night Jesus came to me and told me to help the homeless, just as he said to his friend Peter, "Feed my sheep" (John 21) so many years before.

So I started an educational campaign believing that if people knew about the outrage of homelessness, surely the problem could be solved in a short time. My first major event, complete with a film and speaker, drew four people—three were my good friends and one was the speaker! So I began volunteering every Friday night downtown at the Last Chance Shelter and serving meals at the nearby New Covenant Pentecostal Tabernacle Church of God in Christ soup kitchen. I began reading more about Jesus—the Jesus who sought out those who were suffering and who were left on the margins of society, and while I worked to help them, I was being made whole myself.

That same fall I began listening to the new U2 album called *The Joshua Tree*. I'd really liked U2 before, but now I felt that the anthem "I Still Haven't Found What I'm Looking For" explained exactly how my faith had turned from a self-centered certainty (my prayer: Jesus, help me and bless me) to a world-centered questioning (my prayer: Jesus, why do so many people have to suffer this way?). After I traveled to Nicaragua, to Mexico, and to Jamaica to work with and learn about the struggles of third-world countries, songs like "Bullet the Blue Sky" made so much more sense. As I learned about the heroic struggles of the civil rights movement, I sang out joyfully on "Pride (In the Name of Love)." Jesus had found me, and over the years since then I met him again and again as I listened to the music of U2 and tried to follow Jesus in working with the suffering and outcast of society.

Icons of the Cross

In all the promotional photos for their recent album *How to Dismantle an Atomic Bomb*, the Edge has on a white t-shirt with black crosses all over it. If the image of the cross in association with U2 were unusual, I would pass over it. But whether it is the Edge's shirt or the commonplace sight of Bono's rosary (a beaded necklace with Jesus on the cross as the pendant, given to him by Pope John Paul II in exchange for Bono's blue glasses), the cross is a regular feature in their lyrics and attire. The band very often reveals their faith without speaking of their faith. That is, they use songs and symbols. As Bono says, they "draw their fish in the sand." One easy way to describe this is to speak of U2 as an icon.

"Icon" is an easy enough term. Of course, you might think of "icon" as referring to a sort of "classic," a person who perfectly represents a certain lifestyle. Tommy Hilfiger might be seen as an icon of fashion or Madonna as an icon of pop music. Yet so far, this definition doesn't point enough beyond our love of material success to fully say what I mean by "icon."

Another similar way we use the term "icon" is with the little symbolic pictures on computer desktops. These are icons because the picture refers to a program usually stored on the computer's hard drive. The icon is a shortcut to that program. But the icon in this sense also represents and points to the company that makes the hardware or software and thus works as a marketing tool as well. Here, the definition pushes beyond our association with human material success but still refers to a material point of reference.

What both of these previous definitions miss is something that the original use of icons within the traditions of Eastern Orthodox Christianity called "soul." Rowan Williams, the Archbishop of Canterbury and a scholar of the Eastern Church, has said, "'Soul' is—at least—a religious style of talking about selfhood." Traditionally speaking, an icon is a picture that shows a scene, a person, or a group of persons in a distinctive light, a light that both shows the picture in a strange light and at the same time a light that makes the fullest sense of the meaning of the picture. It is, in a sense, the view of the soul.

The title of this book, *One Step Closer*, raises the question "To What?" The song referred to in the title says, "One step closer to knowing." I view U2 as an icon; that is, I see the band as pointing fans one step closer to the light that is the view of the soul. I do this because I think such a perspective makes a wider, fuller sense of the meaning of the band's words and lives. Thus, I will argue, U2 is an icon that points those who have eyes to see and ears to hear, leading them "one step closer" to the cross, a place both of suffering because of the world's rejection and violent killing of Jesus, as well as joyful hope that comes from God's raising him to new life as a victory over violence, hatred, and death.

As Bono famously wrote: "You broke the bonds and you loosed the chains, carried the cross, all my shame, all my shame, you know I believe it." Yet we live in the space between.

17

While God raised Jesus to life as a sign of the promised "new heaven and a new earth," or as Bono described it "the kingdom come when all the colors bleed into one," this time has yet not arrived. So we sing with Bono, "but I still haven't found what I'm looking for." While we await the return of Jesus and a healing of the nations, we are not surprised by the suffering of the world, but we are not satisfied to allow suffering to continue either, for we have had a glimpse of God's promised future.

The danger is always that the strange light that makes an icon more than what it first appears can be misinterpreted, or even missed altogether. As the nations of Western Europe and North America become more pluralistic, and with an increasing number of young people who have no associations with the Christian faith at all, we might even speak of a cultural loss of soul. If it is the case that fewer people have deep resonance with the Bible and the tradition of the Christian church, then it is also likely the case that many people have lost the ability to see the soul that animates U2. It is tempting to let U2 mean many different things to all manner of spiritual seekers. And of course this is true: the songs and lives of U2 do mean many things to many people. Yet their lives and music make little sense without one central focus, and that central focus is very particular: the cross of Jesus Christ, who was killed by being nailed to a cross in Roman-occupied Palestine in about the year AD 26. That story, told in the Bible, is the light that this book tries to shine around U2 in an effort to show that in various ways their lives and lyrics are indeed an attempt to point fans one step closer to knowing.

Looking Forward

Here I just want to wrap up the introduction by pointing forward through the remainder of the book. Think of it as a map, mainly put here so that you can have a sense of the whole as you read each part. This is especially important, I think, because the book by design is not mainly about U2. Sure, I talk about U2 all the way through, but the point is to help those of you who, when asked if you've ever gone to church, immediately think of the last time you went to a U2 concert! Not that I'm opposed to that; to the contrary, I think the spiritual character of their live shows is one of the most powerful things about U2. But the book is to help you see them as icons, that is, to see them in a fuller light within a complex and often caricatured tradition: Christianity.

In Step One of the book I'll pick up the question of how we talk about God. This question gives a sense of the distinctive "voices" speaking out of Christianity that lead some to talk about various Christianities, as if there are distinct versions of this global faith. I don't particularly want to catalog all modes and models of Christian speech. First of all, that would be boring. Instead, I'm interested in thinking through the kinds of voices used by U2. I'll look in on the ancient patterns of speech found in scripture and show how U2 uses these same patterns in their music.

Step Two of the book circles around the question of how we talk about God. This time, however, I draw on the theology of the cross—a way of speaking of God with deep traditional roots. The theology of the cross might seem an unlikely style to assign to the world's greatest rock and roll band, but these four Dublin men have almost ruined their career in music because of their inability to let go of this way of speaking. It is a way of speaking—or in the case of U2, singing—truthfully and unflinchingly about God and the world God loves. It is a way of speaking that highlights faith over certainty, hope over despair, selfless love over the self-indulgent pursuits that tempt even the church and its leaders to grab power and money for themselves. Most of all, this is a tradition that lives the questions, and it is as quick to critique the church as to critique the world.

Step Three of the book introduces the idea of living the truth as a way to live the cross. To make the theology of the cross clearer as well as livelier, I'll give an account of how U2 "walks its talk," so to speak, in describing how, for U2, following God means *doing* the truth. That, I hope, compels others to seek the truth and to act on the truth in their lives.

STEP ONE . . .

1

SINGING SCRIPTURE

> Words and music did for me what solid, even rigorous
> religious argument could never do, they introduced me to
> God, not belief in God, more an experiential sense of GOD.
> Over art, literature, reason, the way in to my spirit was a
> combination of words and music. As a result the book of
> *Psalms* always felt open to me and led me to the poetry of
> *Ecclesiastes*, the *Song of Solomon*, the book of *John* . . .
>
> Bono, *Introduction to the Psalms*

Beyond "40"

One clear indication that Bono and U2 know the scriptures well is that they sing in the same phrases and patterns as the scriptures. U2 often borrows lyrics straight from the Bible—a practice most clearly exemplified on their 1983 album *War*, which closes with the song "40" taken from Psalm 40 and a refrain from Psalm 6. Like many U2 fans, I was drawn into thinking about the connections of their songs to the Bible through their practice of closing concerts with "40." The feeling of a crowd of thousands singing "how long to sing this song" at the top of their lungs is awesome, sending shivers down my spine in a way that, if I may be honest, happens less often than I'd like in church. If you have attended one of those concerts, or even if you've only heard it on their first live album, *Under a Blood Red Sky*, you understand the incredible connection U2 makes through this simple revival of an ancient psalm. The crowd goes on and on singing "how long to sing this song," long after U2's four members have left the concert hall and said goodnight.

If U2 had only recorded Psalm 40 on an album and then used it as a standard concert closer for a number of years it would have been remarkable in the world of rock and roll. Yet their creative use of Psalm 40 is only the tip of the iceberg as I begin this section considering the role of scripture in the studio and live music of U2 over the years. Many songs include either direct quotations or allusions to specific passages of scripture. For example, in the powerful live performances of "The End of the World" from their early 1990s album *Achtung Baby*, Bono plays the part of Judas and the Edge plays the role of Jesus as they explore this great story of desire and betrayal from the Gospel of Mark, chapter 14. And on their 2004 album *How To Dismantle an Atomic Bomb*, the song "Crumbs from Your Table" is a direct reference to parables from the Gospels of Matthew, chapter 15, and Luke, chapter 16, that set a tone for the song as a whole.

They've quoted the scriptures all along in songs, interviews, and in live performances, but the influence of scripture runs deeper still. The scriptures have so deeply shaped the way they speak that the quotation marks often fall away. The scriptures offer poetic modes of truthful speech about God and the world. Without a sense of the wideness and wildness of the

Bible, you can still love U2 as a great rock and roll band. Yet without that sense of scripture in U2's work, you would miss how, again and again, U2 is pointing beyond themselves to a deeper dimension of life, the dimension of the soul, where one meets face to face with, in Bono's words, "a force of love and logic behind the universe."

Drawing Their Fish in the Sand

One of the most common icons for Jesus is the symbol of the fish. This symbol has been used since the earliest Christian communities, and it is found among the oldest Christian art in the catacombs where Christians gathered to worship during times of persecution. The symbol recalls Jesus's acts of feeding the many people who came to him hungering for food, mercy, healing, and a vision of a renewed and just society. The symbol recalls as well the moments when Jesus visited the disciples after his resurrection. In some accounts, Jesus asked the disciples for fish to eat (John 21). They gave it to him in disbelief at his living presence standing and eating before them. From ancient catacomb art to depictions in stained glass and stone sculpture in grand cathedrals to small fish decals glued to the back of cars, this symbol has stood for centuries as an icon pointing to Jesus Christ.

Angela Pancella, a lead writer for the fabulous U2 fan website @U2.com, created a section of the site titled "Drawing Their Fish in the Sand." She tops the column dedicated to scriptural references in U2 songs with this quote from Bono:

We've found different ways of expressing [our faith], and recognized the power of the media to manipulate such signs. Maybe we just have to sort of draw our fish in the sand. It's

25

there for people who are interested. It shouldn't be there for people who aren't.

Bono's reference makes sense once one understands a bit of church history.

During the early years of the Christian church there were waves of harsh persecution by the Romans. At these times, it was dangerous to be public about one's Christian faith. As a protection, when a Christian met someone new, he or she would draw a single arc in the sand. If the other person was a Christian, he or she would complete the drawing of a fish with the second arc. If the second person was not a Christian, the ambiguity of the drawing would not reveal the first person as a person of faith.

A glance down the list of scriptural quotes and allusions in songs from "I Will Follow" to "Grace" makes clear that although U2 is deeply shaped by the world of scripture, they also commonly use scripture in such a way that their songs are iconic, pointing toward deeper things, toward the soul, rather than speaking directly and simply about issues of faith as so much of contemporary Christian music does.

This means that U2's songs are multi-layered, written in modes of poetry and accessible from many angles, not all of them dependent on seeing "the fish in the sand." While one might catch direct references to God, Jesus, and other explicitly religious themes, more often than not they write out of the world of scripture implicitly—that is, without explicit religious terms or quotations from the Bible—in order to speak the truth they see in the world. Bono put it this way:

> I enjoy the test of trying to keep hold of what's sacred, and still being awake, walking around, breaking through the plate glass window. It's one thing being in that holy huddle; it's another thing taking yourself out there into the world.

26

So often Christians fall into the trap of only speaking about the world of scripture. Bono, on the other hand, reminds us that the scripture is not about itself, but about mixed up people seeking to look at the world through the eyes of love, as God does. And in large part, Bono draws on scripture at its most powerful; that is, he draws upon its poetry.

It ought to be said, therefore, that rather than providing a distraction from the world, poetry lends itself to telling the truth about the world, and this is exactly what makes scripture so dynamic as a force shaping the songs of U2. It is not the kind of truth telling offered in math. That 2+2=4 is true has clear meaning for us and is not the subject of much debate. As biblical scholar Ellen Davis writes, the Bible's poets tell truth in a different way. They seek "to open the world to us through the artful use of words. They invite us to be patient and curious about the word choices they make. They speak to us at multiple levels, in suggestive ways, rather than through rational explanations." Part one of this book is intended to make us ask questions about the word choices U2 makes as they draw from scripture and how these word choices open the truth of God's world.

Modes of Scripture's Voice

While U2 has changed over time in the way they draw on scripture in their songs, many key emphases have remained constant. For instance, the song "40" hints at how profound the voice of the psalms has been for U2. Their songbook is, to some fans, the embodiment of a contemporary book of psalms, full of the honesty and passion that fills the psalms of old. Prophetic speech, too, has been there from early on. This mode was present in early live performances of "Sunday Bloody Sunday," with Bono running around stage waving a

27

white flag to symbolize the song's call for the end of fighting and the coming of a hoped-for peace. But the 1990s found them shifting from the mixture of the sacred and erotic in Proverbs and the Song of Songs to an embrace of irony and life's vanity in Ecclesiastes. And their latest work simply shows a maturing of vision that reveals complex, layered visions that draw on the voices of scripture in profound and provocative ways.

In the next few chapters, then, I offer brief interpretations of the major voices of scripture that echo in U2's songs. Singing scripture has offered a powerful way for the band to speak truthfully about the complex reality of both desiring God and yet looking full on at the world in all its messiness. In each chapter, I'll offer a brief section that describes the shape of each particular voice—psalms, wisdom, prophecy, parable, and apocalypse—and then show how in each case this voice of scripture gives shape to a couple of U2's songs.

People for whom the Bible is strange territory may find this approach to see through U2's songs to the world of scripture off-putting. That is fine for now. I invite you to suspend judgment and come with me on this journey. I'll do my best to show I'm not reading scripture into songs where it doesn't belong, but rather highlighting an important aspect of these songs in order to gain a deeper appreciation of them. The Bible, despite its reputation in some circles, is not a "rule book" for the moral judgments of the fundamentalists. The Bible is actually a wild place, full of flawed heroes, the worst villains, powerful poetry, and that most amazing reality of all at the center of it—grace.

2

PSALMS AS THANKSGIVING AND LAMENT

The Psalter may be a font of gospel music, but for me it's in his despair that the psalmist really reveals the nature of his special relationship with God. Honesty, even to the point of anger. "How long, Lord? Wilt though hide thyself forever?" (Psalm 89) or "Answer me when I call" (Psalm 5).

Bono, *Introduction to the Psalms*

What Are Psalms?

The brilliance of the psalms is that they speak of our whole existence before God. Psalms are earthy and therefore don't hurry past the reality of human experience. Rather, they dwell deeply in the midst of life, taking seriously the raw energy of human agony and ecstasy. The honesty of feeling abandoned echoes through Psalm 22:

God, God . . . My God!
Why did you dump me miles from nowhere?
Doubled up with pain, I call to God all the day long.
No answer. Nothing.

And the clear exuberance of feeling God's blessing flows out
in joy and gratitude in Psalm 116:

What can I give back to God
for the blessings he's poured out on me?
I'll lift high the cup of salvation—a toast to God!
I'll pray in the name of God;
I'll complete what I promised God I'd do,
and I'll do it together with his people.

Lament and thanksgiving, agony and ecstasy, are a way of
summing up all of life by pointing to its full range of experience. Everything, according to the psalmist, can be brought
before God.

The psalms find their foundational voice in thanksgiving.
Yet more than a third of all psalms can be categorized as lament psalms, psalms full of pain, anger, and abandonment.
This is not because Israel's God was disengaged from the
world, looking down on the world with curious amusement.
Rather, Israel's God is the God who acts in history. Israel
became a people through the experience of liberation from
oppression. God heard their cries, brought them up out of
slavery in Egypt, and gave them a future full of hope and
joy. There is, therefore, under almost every cry of lament,
an undercurrent of faith that because this awesome God can
make a way out of no way, hope for God's presence and action is not in vain.

Psalm 40 is among the best places for us to turn for an example of thanksgiving for God's past action intertwined with

lament about some current circumstances. One who does not know the goodness of God does not turn to God in lament. Why bother? Psalm 40, therefore, begins with thanksgiving for God's help in the past:

> I waited and waited and waited for God.
>> At last he looked; finally he listened.
> He lifted me out of the ditch,
>> pulled me from deep mud.
> He stood me up on a solid rock
>> to make sure I wouldn't slip.

One can imagine here the people's long memory back to the clay pits of Egypt where the slaves worked making bricks to support the Pharaoh's building campaign (Exodus 1–3). They indeed waited and waited and waited. But their historical memory is not of abandonment but of waiting and deliverance. That is foundational to Israel's faith. God hears and acts. The movement of the psalms from the minor key of complaint to the major chord of thanksgiving echoes the lives of God's people.

Who has not been in such a depressed and hopeless place? In such a place you wake in the morning only to feel the lead weight of trouble settle down on your shoulders, a weight only shaken off again by the next night of restless sleep. To find release from such a place, to gain solid footing again after feeling like everything is sinking, is truly to understand salvation. It is no wonder that as the psalmist recalls God's help in the past, he remembers that it evoked a new song, a fresh moment. After a night of weeping, joy came in the morning. The psalmist continues:

> He taught me how to sing the latest God-song,
>> a praise-song to our God.

31

God not only lets the oppressed go free, he also gives them the gift of music, teaching them to celebrate, to sing and to dance. Such rejoicing after a particularly difficult time is the sweetest delight.

But our reading of Psalm 40 thus far only takes us halfway through the psalm. The memory of suffering and God's deliverance that gives rise to songs of thanksgiving serves as a solace in the trials of the present. It is here, in the moment, when God's power is needed but seemingly absent, that the full force of lament comes into play. As we read on in Psalm 40, the voice changes from past to present, from thanksgiving for past help to lament for present troubles.

> When troubles ganged up on me,
>   a mob of sins past counting,
> I was so swamped by guilt
>   I couldn't see my way clear.
> More guilt in my heart than hair on my head,
>   so heavy the guilt that my heart gave out.
> Soften up, God, and intervene;
>   hurry and get me some help.

We don't know the source of the guilt here confessed. We don't know if it was an individual alone or a representative of the people lamenting common guilt. But it is possible because of this generality to enter in with our own troubles and failings and to feel our own heart grow faint. Even the agnostic who prays in a crisis "just to cover her bases" can relate to the elemental prayer of "help." While many people inside and outside of the church might think only eloquent prayers and holy lives are acceptable to God, the psalms show that to be patently false. Feeling overwhelmed and shouting out, "Hurry and get me some help" seems nearer to the ordinary desperation anyone might feel in a pinch.

Psalm 40 is a faithful lament. It is the voice of those who know God's goodness but find the troubles of the present moment nearly overwhelming. Such a lament, sung in our midst, does not solve anything, really. But so much of life's trouble has no easy solution. So learning to sing songs of faithful lament helps us to give voice to our experience together, before God. The long space between our cries and God's answer is not simply a modern experience formed by the doubt of various kinds of atheism and denial of God's power to act. Rather, this path of patient longing is well worn by the footsteps of these ancestors in the faith who brought their doubts, suffering, and even outright anger before the God whom they knew to be faithful regardless of how things looked at the moment.

How Long?

The version of Psalm 40 sung by U2 was the last song on their third record, *War*. As the title indicates, the record in part attempts to respond to violence — in Northern Ireland and, more generally, the global preoccupation with nuclear war during the 1970s and 1980s. On the last song, "40," they beautifully render this psalm's mood of faithful lament. The chorus combines thanksgiving's "new song" with lament's cry "how long." This paradoxical chorus holds together the essential memory of Israel's experience of faith: that even if we know and believe that God has acted to save those who cry out under oppression, our current sorrow knows no such easy rescue.

The paradox of lament and thanksgiving together is especially poignant when one contrasts "40," the last track on *War*, to the first song, "Sunday Bloody Sunday." The Edge came up with the idea for the song as a cry against violence. Its name comes from an infamous event on Sunday, January

30, 1972, in Derry, Ireland. On that day, British soldiers from a parachute regiment shot and killed thirteen unarmed people participating in a demonstration. The soldiers were cleared under the pretense that some in the crowd had shot at them first. Staccato drums begin the song, recalling the marching beat of political marches in Ireland. The song's first lines call to mind the shock of hearing of another horrific act: "I can't believe the news today / I can't close my eyes and make it go away." While the song has clear links to events in Derry, it takes up the theme of violence and suffering in a more general way, as well, lamenting the "trenches dug within our hearts" and calling out in a repeated refrain — "How long, how long must we sing this song?"

"Sunday Bloody Sunday" asks the psalmist's question in a strident and impatient voice, almost in a shout. Indeed, Bono has often shifted off the lyrics midway, taking up a chorus of shouts, alternating between his singing and the audience's "No More, No More, No More, No More." And as he does this, Bono has often run around the stage with a white flag — a flag of surrender. Like so many lament psalms, this song anticipates hope because of God's past and promised actions. The idea of the song, Bono said in a recent interview, "was to contrast Bloody Sunday, where 13 peaceful Irish protesters were killed by British paratroopers, with an Easter Sunday. I had started to discover the principle of nonviolence at the time, and there's a piece of that in there." According to Christian teaching, on Easter Sunday, God rejected the horrific violence of humans toward one another by raising Jesus from the tomb. "The real battle just begun / to claim the victory Jesus won . . ." is a rallying cry to join God's way of nonviolence.

But while the original version juxtaposed Bloody Sunday with Easter Sunday, with its intentionally hopeful and empowering ending, another direction is also possible. One occasion when Bono sang this elaborated version of "Sunday Bloody Sunday" in a concert at Slane Castle, Ireland, in 2001 (later made into a concert DVD), the song ends with Bono listing names, one after the other:

> Sunday bloody Sunday / Breda / Sunday bloody Sunday / Sean / Sunday bloody Sunday / Julie / Sunday bloody Sunday / Gareth / Sunday bloody Sunday / Sean
>
> Sunday bloody Sunday / Geraldine / Sunday bloody Sunday / Jolene
>
> Philomena Skelton / Gareth Conway / Breda Devine / Lorraine Wilson / (The music stops here) Samantha McFaraland / Julia Hughes / Elizabeth Rush / Rico Abad-Amos / Fernando Blasco Baselga / Esther Gibson /Ann McCombe / Veda Short /
>
> Adrian Gallagher/ Alan Rudford / Fred White / His son Brian White / Brian McCrory / Sean McGrath / 29 people / Too many

The guitar and bass immediately pick up a slow and careful tune, mournful and full of soul. A single spotlight catches Bono wandering slowly around the stage and then finally sitting down. He picks up the vocal from the closing song on their 1997 album *Pop*, "Wake Up Dead Man"

> "Jesus / Jesus help me / I'm alone in this world / and a f**ked up world it is, too / Tell me, tell me the story, the one about eternity /and how its all gonna be / Wake up / Wake up, dead man."

One of the most haunting songs of lament, sung here as a response to one of the most haunting acts of violence in recent years in Ireland. The list of names comes from the heinous

1998 bombing at Omagh, Ireland. The bomb, planted at a shopping center by the splinter group the Real IRA, was aimed at stopping the Good Friday Accords that at the time offered the most concrete possibility of peace in Northern Ireland. In the face of such random violence, U2 offers what is perhaps their most raw and plaintive lament psalm.

In turning to this darker lament form, U2 picks up on the theme of God's seeming absence clearly present in the psalms. As Brian Walsh has well noted, "Wake Up, Dead Man" draws on Psalm 44 as a model for such a cry of desperation and abandonment.

> Get up, God! Are you going to sleep all day?
>> Wake up! Don't you care what happens to us?
> Why do you bury your face in the pillow?
>> Why pretend things are just fine with us?
> And here we are—flat on our faces in the dirt,
>> held down with a boot on our necks.
> Get up and come to our rescue.
>> If you love us so much, *Help us!*

The inquisitive complaint of this psalm could have come from any of us. It is the feeling of a child who has been hurt while the parent's careful attention was distracted. It is the cry of people who experience the harm humans can cause one another, and yet find no relief but only pain. No pretty poetry or flowery language required to address God here—just plain, direct, and angry words: "Don't you care?"

Christians, like the Jews, live between promise and fulfillment. Just as Jews await the Messiah and the fulfillment his return will bring, so Christians await the return of Christ when the new age begun through his death and resurrection will be brought to fulfillment. Then, we believe, Isaiah's vision of a new heaven and a new earth, of no tears and no sadness, of food and drink for all will be made reality. Yet we live in a time of the long in-between when we know the power of the promise and yet still see the result of the old earth, full of tears and sadness, where some eat and drink to excess while others starve. This is our reality. Lament is the outcry of the overwhelmed.

And yet, lament is a moment of being overwhelmed *within the life of faith*. Intermixed into the song "Wake Up, Dead Man" we find clear statements of faith. "Jesus, I'm waiting here, boss / I know you're looking out for us / But maybe your hands aren't free." Here, we are depicted as waiting in faith that Jesus does look out for us. But, if so, why do we suffer our current troubles? "Your Father, He made the world in seven / He's in charge of heaven / Will you put a word in for me?" Here, God's power to create the world in seven days and his Lordship of heaven are seemingly not enough to gain some help, and the song pleads with Jesus to bend God's ear for some special consideration. The fundamental truth that life is not fair causes such complaint. We ask, "Why me? Why now? That was the last thing I need today!"

Yet beyond Psalm 44, the song echoes another passage that gives some indication of U2's response to such questioning of God's seeming absence, and it gives a clue to their way of getting out of such despair. The image comes from a short passage from the Gospel of Matthew, chapter 8, when Jesus and his disciples are crossing the Sea of Galilee. They get out on the lake and a sudden storm blows in. The waves begin crashing into the boat. Jesus was below deck sleeping, worn out from the crowds pressing all around him seeking healing and help of every kind. The disciples lose their cool in the face of the storm and they run down under the deck shouting, "Wake up, Jesus. We're going down!" Jesus wakes up, and he scolds them: "Why are you such cowards, such faint-hearts?" Then he told the wind to be silent and the sea to quiet down.

Jesus, apparently, didn't want his disciples to solely depend on him, but rather to stand upon their own faith. He wants to pass on to them the faith that moves mountains. He wants them to be bold in the face of the storms of life. He teaches them by example, and tutors them by prophecy and parables and then — at times — even spells it out in plain prose. He is, in fact, asking why they have so little faith. He wants them to act. He wants them to claim their participation in God's breaking into the world that Jesus's life represents.

And here we catch something of the spirituality of U2. A response to lament is participation in God's work in the world. Bono put it thus, "A pastor recently told me, 'Stop asking God to bless what you are doing. Find out what God's doing. It's already blessed.' That's what I want. I want to align my life with that." This fits with his image that rather than being kicked out of paradise by God, we kicked God out by trying to live there by ourselves. Only when we're mature enough to admit how badly we've screwed it up are we able to see our need for grace. Then, with grace as a cover for our ugliness, we see the world as a place where God is already working through the Spirit to make things new. Then, found by grace, we can join up with God in order to restore a sense of sanity to the world. Rather than simply saying it directly, though, as if taking up God's work in the world were as simple as answering the appeal of the TV preacher, U2 points as an icon to something beyond. Toward the end of "Wake Up Dead Man," they point to the mysterious presence of God over, in, and through the things of this world:

> Listen to the words they'll tell you what to do / Listen over the rhythm that's confusing you / Listen to the reed in the saxophone / Listen over the hum of the radio / Listen over the sound of blades in rotation / Listen through the traffic and

circulation / Listen as hope and peace try to rhyme / Listen over marching bands playing out their time.

Lament, grounded in thanksgiving's faith, looks beyond itself toward prophetic action. "Wake Up Dead Man" is not finally a song of resignation. Not at the last. It is a hymn of faithful doubt, a lament grounded in thanksgiving. It is a song that resists the urge to throw in the towel and say, "Forget it. He's dead. He can't help us now." Rather, the song turns on insistence, even persistence: "Wake up! Listen! Help!"

When we pray the psalms, and especially the laments, we trust that despite our feelings of loss, pain, and abandonment, we are not alone. Christians believe that Jesus prays with us in suffering because he is no stranger to the betrayal, suffering, and abandonment we feel. On the cross, he prayed in the words of Psalm 22: "My God, my God, why have you abandoned me?" As Dietrich Bonhoeffer, the German pastor killed for resistance to Hitler, wrote from prison: "Now we know that there is no longer any suffering on earth in which Christ will not be with us, suffering with us and praying with us—Christ the only helper." On this basis, we have hope. It is not a false hope that God will rescue us from all trials and make everything okay. Rather we have a real hope that God is in the midst of life, suffering and working with us to bring into being that life we only know from a promise and see in glimpses.

The experience of such a promise, such a glimpse of how things are supposed to be, comes perhaps, for U2 and for many U2 fans, in live concerts. Many fans, as I mentioned in the introduction, think of U2 live as a religious experience or even "like church" only so much better. This may make traditionalists nervous, but there is a reason for such a feeling. The 2001 Elevation tour offers a great example of such an experience. For this tour, the main set closed with "Where the Streets Have No Name." For example, in the Live from Boston concert (available on DVD), Bono leads the crowd singing "40," which the crowd sings until the Edge comes in with the classic beginning sounds of "Streets." As this guitar intro continues, Bono speaks:

> What can I give back to God / for the blessings he poured out on me? / What can I give back to God / for the blessings he poured out on me? / I lift high the cup of Salvation / as a toast to our Father / To follow through on a promise / I made to you from the heart.

Then a long "Oooooooowhaaaaaaa" from Bono and the band kicks into full drive as he begins to sing the song's actual lyrics "I want to run / I want to hide." What's going on here? Some people wondered if Bono was just improvising. But, it turned out, that concert after concert and city after city Bono was actually quoting directly from Psalm 116 as translated in Eugene Peterson's *The Message: The Bible in Contemporary Language* (a version of the Bible Bono loves). This is the introduction to a song that has, in at least one main interpretation of its meaning, to do with heaven, the New Jerusalem, a place truly where the streets have no name (see more on this song below in chapter six). It is a simple act of praise and thanksgiving rooted in profound gratitude for the life they live. It is, finally, what the psalms are meant to do—bring our lives, our whole lives, before God, whose gift and promised life is in the beginning.

Additional U2 Psalms of Thanksgiving and Lament

"Gloria, With A Shout," "Scarlet" (*October*); "Drowning Man" (*War*); "MLK" (*The Unforgettable Fire*); "Mothers of the

Disappeared" (*The Joshua Tree*); "Love is Blindness" (*Achtung Baby*); "The First Time" (*Zooropa*); "Peace on Earth" (*All That You Can't Leave Behind*); "Yahweh" (*How to Dismantle an Atomic Bomb*)

Others?

3

WISDOM AS DESIRE
AND ILLUSION

It took U2 fifteen years to get from Psalms to
Ecclesiastes. And it's only one book!

Bono

What Is Wisdom?

Wisdom, like the psalms, speaks of the full stretch of living.
At times wisdom seems like an influential first-grade teacher
or favorite uncle who helped put us on life's path:

Don't be quick to fly off the handle.
Anger Boomerangs. You can spot a fool by the lumps on his
head. (Ecclesiastes 7)

Yet in Song of Songs, wisdom writing takes full measure of
the pleasure that awaits us beyond childhood:

43

The sweet, fragrant curves of your body,
    the soft, spiced contours of your flesh
Invite me, and I come. I stay
    until dawn breaths its light and night slips away. (4)

And to bring the trajectory of wisdom full circle, Ecclesiastes faces death straight on:

In old age, your body no longer serves you so well.
Muscles slacken, grip weakens, joints stiffen.
The shades are pulled down on the world.
You can't come and go at will. Things grind to a halt. (12)

Like the psalms, nothing human is strange to the voice of wisdom in scripture.

Yet wisdom's voice is distinct from the main voice of the psalms in exactly how explicit this literature references God. While God is ever present, the traditional books of wisdom literature in the Bible—Song of Songs, Proverbs, and Ecclesiastes—don't speak of God much at all. These books, however, are wisdom because they inquire so deeply and so persistently after the fundamental question of how to live a life that honors God. It is a perspective on honoring God that moves through poetic language to express the wisdom learned through experience. Such wisdom may have its origin in God, but wisdom literature focuses less on its divine origin and more on its self-evident truth. In this way, wisdom evokes responses in the reader, asking us to ponder if, indeed, our experience leads us to similar insights.

Although the wisdom literature has had periods of intense popularity (especially in medieval times), it is among the least known and infrequently read portions of scripture in Christian churches today. Eugene Peterson suggests why: "It is fairly common among people who get interested in religion or God to get proportionally *dis*interested in their jobs and families, their communities and their colleagues—the more of God, the less of the human." From this perspective, to the extent that one embraces the earthy perspective of wisdom writings, the more one distances oneself from God. But, Peterson warns, this is just not so. If anything, these writings are essential because of "Wisdom's unrelenting insistence that nothing in human experience can be omitted or slighted if we decide to take God seriously and respond to him believingly." Exactly because of its insistence on dealing with the mundane matters of daily life, much can be gained from wisdom writings.

Wisdom literature has had a distinctive influence beyond the books of the Bible most often placed under that designation. I'll summarize those broadly influential impulses with the words desire and illusion. First, desire. Desire comes in the obvious sense of sensuality in the love poetry of Song of Songs. This book does not contain a single overt reference to God, yet its strong echoes of the biblical stories show it to be a profound and elaborate portrayal of the Garden of Eden restored and made whole again. Eden, after all, means delight—a term used over and over in Song of Songs. But the delight of this beautiful book is its multilayered meaning framed in delicious poetic language. The writing is deeply theological, and yet it is also what it seems on the surface—a celebration of human love and desire.

Desire comes in a less obvious guise in Proverbs, where wisdom takes on the form of a distinguished woman. Lady Wisdom, as she is often called, makes her entry in the beginning of Proverbs:

> Lady Wisdom goes out in the street and shouts.
> At the town center she makes her speech.

The theme continues in chapter 8, but with even more energy:

> Do you hear Lady Wisdom calling?
>   Can you hear Madame Insight raising her voice?
> She's taken her stand at First and Main,
>   at the busiest intersection.
> Right in the city square
>   where traffic is thickest, she shouts,
> "You—I'm talking to all of you,
>   everyone out here on the streets!
> Listen, you idiots—learn good sense!
>   You blockheads—shape up!
> Don't miss a word of this—I'm telling you how to live well,
>   I'm telling you how to live at your best."

She speaks with authority, calling all who will listen to live according to God's will.

She gains this authority by her partnership with God. Later in chapter 8, she reports "God sovereignly made me—the first, the basic—before he did anything else." Since from the beginning she "was right there with him, making sure everything fit," she claims authority in asking the reader to "listen to me." She promises, "When you find me, you find life, real life." She is to be highly desired for this life she offers. In some cases, she is portrayed as beautiful and a worthy object of desire. Other times, the life she offers is portrayed as a great banquet meal that she sets for all those who are "confused about life," who "don't know what's going on." To them, she says in chapter 9, "Come with me, oh come, have dinner with me!" "Leave your impoverished confusion and *live!*"

Many commentators make connections between Lady Wisdom and other portions of scripture. First, given her description of being with God at the creation, one might see an echo of wisdom in God's Spirit brooding over the waters at the creation (Genesis 1). But even more important are the many references to wisdom in the narratives of Jesus's life. In many cases, these stories about Jesus draw directly from Proverbs, including multiple invitations to banquet meals that symbolize God's kingdom of life. Perhaps none is so relevant as Jesus's discussion with Nicodemus about baptism and new life (see the Gospel of John, chapter 3). Jesus had described the need to be "born from above" in response to Nicodemus's question about Jesus's power and teaching. Nicodemus questions how someone who has been born and is now grown can be born again. And Jesus, recalling the spirit's hovering over the waters of creation, speaks of being shaped by something one cannot see or touch—the Spirit. And Jesus then goes on to describe the freedom of the Spirit to blow where she will, here or there (echoing the creation story from Genesis, but also Ecclesiastes 8: "No one can control the wind or lock it in a box"). Nicodemus's problem, Jesus implies, is that of the people wisdom addresses: he does not recognize his ignorance and does not desire what the Spirit offers to him—life, new life, abundant life!

A second influential theme within the wisdom writings is illusion—or even disillusionment. This is the voice of Ecclesiastes and its author, often translated "the Preacher" or "the Quester." The book, like life, is full of contradictions and a sometimes rather cynical dismissal of life's supposed meaningfulness. Here life is stripped down in the search for meaning, tested and found wanting in most areas that the young and the naïve imagine will prove valuable. The book opens with that famous negative judgment, "Smoke, nothing but smoke. . . . There's nothing to anything—it's all smoke." After this auspicious beginning, the Quester embarks on the story of a journey seeking the good life.

47

> With the help of a bottle of wine
> and all the wisdom I could muster,
> I tried my level best
> to penetrate the absurdity of life. (2)

The Quester tries it all—money, entertainment, sex—and found it all unsatisfactory.

> Everything I wanted I took—I never said no to myself. I gave in to every impulse, held back nothing. I sucked the marrow of pleasure out of every task—my reward to myself for a hard day's work! (2)

The result? "Smoke and spitting into the wind. There was nothing to any of it. Nothing."

Yet in the midst of this relentless questioning of all life offers, the Quester holds together the steely-eyed lancing of all pride and ambition with a deeper truth.

> But against all illusion and fantasy and empty talk
> There's always this rock foundation: Fear God! (5)

Why, however, should one fear God after facing the bitter truth that all ambition and achievement in this life is smoke?

> After looking at the way things are on this earth, here's what I've decided is the best way to live: Take care of yourself, have a good time, and make the most of whatever job you have for as long as God gives you life. And that's about it. (5)

Yet, taking this life philosophy one step further, the Quester does admit that we do, after all, have a role to play in making the world a place we want to live in. "I did spot one ray of light in this murk: God made men and women true and upright; *we're* the ones who've made a mess of things" (7).

Ellen Davis, in a lovely and insightful commentary on the books of wisdom writing, suggests that this material was written at a time when God's people were experiencing great cultural anxiety and social change after a period of stability and prosperity. The Quester, she writes,

> takes on the anxiety as his own; he feels its full toll on the human spirit. His witness of faith was preserved within circles of Jewish and later Christian piety precisely because of its "dangerous" unconventionality, because he dares to look at radical doubt from the inside and thus speaks to those whom no ordinary assurances could satisfy.

Such a voice, deeply immersed in the life of the world and willing to press for meaning despite anxiety and doubt, makes a powerful partner for those of us living through the last fifteen years in the developed nations of the West. These years have seen dramatic change, with the fall of the Berlin Wall, and with it most of Soviet and Eastern European Communism, and the rise of new tensions provoked by assertions of American military and cultural power around the globe. And this set of tensions—doubt and anxiety, mixed with faith and hope—find a central place in the songs of U2, as well. Let's turn now to a couple examples of wisdom's voice there.

Spirit Moves

When U2 sings a love song, it is usually more than, as Paul McCartney famously put it, just a "silly" love song. U2's friends and fans commonly acknowledge that U2's songs usually have multiple layers of meaning. Love songs, in particular, are commonly about (at least) a woman and about God. This might seem strange to someone who has never read wisdom literature. Yet, in the Christian tradition, Song of Songs represents both a portrait of human love and a vision of the soul's highest goal of passionate love for God. Lady Wisdom is both the giver of life and ultimately lovely and desirable herself. Such longing and desire need not always have sexual overtones, as in Jesus's passionate cry "Jerusalem, Jerusalem, . . . How often I've longed to gather your children, gather your children like a hen, / Her brood safe under her wings—but you refused and turned away!" (Luke 13).

The song arguably strongest in this category is "Mysterious Ways" from 1991's *Achtung Baby*. As a record, *Achtung Baby* is an extended meditation on themes of desire and betrayal. It is also the band's first record of the 1990s, marking the new territory U2 would explore throughout that decade. A (too) simplistic contrast could be made that the 1980s were about love, justice, doubt, and faith. The 1990s, beginning with *Achtung Baby* and the ZooTV tour that followed, marked a shift in their dominant mode of singing with their hearts on their sleeve, as is so characteristic of the psalms. While never leaving behind the psalms, especially the lament, U2 began an experimental phase inspired partly by wisdom literature. Here, they seek God in a more oblique fashion, looking straight on at the world (as in the famous line from *Pop*'s "Mofo," "looking for the baby Jesus under the trash").

"Mysterious Ways" is typically layered with meaning, starting from the first line of the song: "Johnny, take a walk with your sister the moon." The allusion is to Oscar Wilde's one act tragedy *Salomé*, the story of John the Baptist's beheading (see the Gospel of Matthew, chapter 14). The play takes place at the Palace of Herod, where some soldiers are standing outside of the great banquet hall and commenting "Look at the moon.

How strange the moon seems! She is like a woman rising from a tomb." On one level then the "she" in the song's title draws on the symbol of the moon, commonly given both female and divine characteristics in ancient religious traditions. This only gets us part way into a full sense of the song, however.

A second key image is that of Salomé herself, who comes out to talk to John the Baptist and finds him strangely desirable. He strongly rejects her advances and denounces her and her mother. Herod had earlier asked Salomé to dance for him and his guests from Rome. Salomé now agrees, but only with the promise from Herod that she could have whatever she wanted. She dances, and then asks for John the Baptist's head. So, here the theme of desire and betrayal, a theme running throughout *Achtung Baby*, is symbolized in Salomé as one who "moves in mysterious ways." The video for this song shot in Fez, Morocco, features a woman in flowing red robes dancing beautifully and hauntingly. When this song has been played in concert, video footage or an actual dancer has been part of the show. While the idea of having a belly dancer on tour to dance on stage during the song began as a joke on Bono, he actually liked it and it was a standard throughout the ZooTV tour.

The song is not wholly about Salomé, however, and that leads us to a third key image — spirit — that shifts the meaning of the other two — "she" and love — when they are used as virtual equivalents. (For the record, U2 did a song that directly tells the story — "Salomé," which was released as a b-side for the single "Even Better Than The Real Thing" from *Achtung Baby*.) The added theme of the spirit draws straightforwardly on wisdom literature and offers something beyond themes of the moon's haunting beauty and a woman's potential for desire and betrayal. The first hint of this interpretation comes at the end of the first verse: "You've been running away from what you don't understand — love." She/love is the one whose gonna "be there when you hit the ground." She/love will "lift my days, light up my nights." Like Lady Wisdom, she will "talk about the things you can't explain." And as in Proverbs, the one who would reach for the best of life must learn how to sit at Lady Wisdom's feet and learn her ways: "if you want to kiss the sky, better learn how to kneel."

The layers of symbolic language that push past "she" to "love" to "spirit" comes toward the end of the song. Here, Bono shifts from "she moves" to "spirit moves" making the implied spiritual depth of "she" explicit. In the version of the song during the ZooTV tour supporting *Achtung Baby*, Bono riffs on the lyrics making this connection even more clear:

> She moves in mysterious ways / Oh Love, / Mmm, Love / I feel your comfort, love / I need your comfort / Move me Spirit, hold me / Move me Spirit, feed me / Move me Spirit, take me / Move me Spirit, teach me / To move with it, / To move with it, / Lift my days, light up my nights, love.

Such a move in language echoes a number of biblical themes. Most obvious, of course, is the vision of Lady Wisdom as deeply interconnected with God from the beginning, suggesting a feminine aspect of God's power in creation. Less obvious, but integrally related here, is the way Bono draws on the Old Testament name for God, "El Shaddhai." This name is often described as a combination of Elohim, meaning God's power, and a version of Shad, meaning breast. Thus: El Shaddhai as the Powerful Breasted One, the one who feeds and comforts and nourishes the people and makes them fountains of blessing and life as well. In concluding some comments about El Shaddhai as a biblical name for God, Bono remarks, "I've always believed that the spirit is a feminine thing."

The fullest and most obvious sense, however, is the way the song draws on a basic biblical theme of the spirit moving in mysterious ways, a thought drawn from wisdom literature. Bono comments, "You know, it says somewhere in Scripture that the Spirit moves like a wind—no one knows where it's come from or where it's going. The Spirit is described in the Holy Scriptures as much more anarchic than any established religion credits." This sensibility recalls the description of the spirit by Jesus in the Gospel of John, chapter 3, where he says,

> You know well enough how the wind blows this way and that. You hear it rustling through the trees, but you have no idea where it comes from or where it's headed next. That's the way it is with everyone "born from above" by the wind of God, the Spirit of God.

In one sense the song is addressed to a man who has become hardened to love, to feeling, and in another sense, to the experience of the Spirit. The song builds its address, never admitting that such love and feeling would be simple, but rather that she/love/spirit is the ground that holds us and gives us life. Affirmations abound: "One day you'll look back, and you'll see where you were held now by this love."

"Mysterious Ways" models one key mode of U2's singing wisdom, but its hopeful ending notes don't fit with the more disillusioned voice of the Quester who wrote Ecclesiastes. One might argue that songs picking up the voice of the Quester are more typical of the 1990s when U2 worked deliberately to try on masks that enabled them to seek the holy in the mundane, in the places abandoned and condemned by proper society. The Fly (an egomaniacal rock star), MacPhisto (the devil), and Mirrorball Man (a cross between a televangelist and the fat Elvis), all invented stage personae during the 1990s, were a way for Bono to speak in other voices and to mock his own stardom, the absurdity of consumer culture that produces rock stars, and even the devil himself whose offer of power and glittering prizes stand close at hand.

Yet one of the most interesting masks Bono speaks through is the voice of Johnny Cash, who sings the vocal on the concluding song on 1993's *Zooropa*. Titled "The Wanderer," the song was intended to directly echo themes of Ecclesiastes. Their original idea was to call the song "The Preacher," one of the traditional translations of the author of Ecclesiastes. It has overtones of Mirrorball Man and the shallowness of Las Vegas in the tune, played in the fashion of a bad Holiday Inn bar band. But the shallow be-bop and "oo, ooing" of the background vocals clash with the gravity of Cash's powerful voice, raising a musical question about the shallowness of so much of our culture today.

The song draws on the theme of a journey in search of life's meaning, but with a pretty jaded perspective right from the start. "The Wanderer" says, in the first lines, "I went out walking through streets paved with gold / Lifted some stones, saw the skin and bones / Of a city without a soul." Compare this to the beginning of the Quester's journey in the second chapter of Ecclesiastes: "With the help of a bottle of wine and all the wisdom I could muster, I tried my level best to penetrate the absurdity of life." Clearly "The Wanderer" is looking for life's meaning but cynical about how flowery that meaning actually is from various angles. He finds, for instance, citizens sitting outside a church house who "say they want the kingdom, but they don't want God in it." The song literally takes place nowhere — it inhabits a surrealist landscape that calls to mind both science fiction movies and the God-haunted territory of Flannery O'Connor, a Southern American novelist whose writings are favorites of the band. Her writing conventions were shaped to fit the blindness of our age: "to the hard of hearing you shout, and for the almost-blind you draw large and startling figures."

"The Wanderer," then, aims to evoke such a startling figure—a picture or a sketch of strange spiritual restlessness. The lyrics are disturbing in the same way as passages from Ecclesiastes can be disturbing. They force a questioning of where truth is found. The closing lines could describe the 1990s as a whole for U2 as they wander among the symbols of a frenzied media and commercial culture yet all the while seeking something redeeming beneath it.

> Now Jesus, don't you wait up, Jesus I'll be home soon. / Yeah, I went out for the papers, told her I'd be back by noon. / Yeah, I left with nothing but the thought you'd be there too / Looking for you. / Yeah, I went with nothing, nothing but the thought of you. / I went wandering.

It is ultimately a faithful journey, but the clarity is refracted; our journey toward truth is often a winding and convoluted path and what we find at the end is not always the truth we expected at the beginning of the journey.

Additional U2 Songs Drawing on Wisdom Themes

"A Sort of Homecoming, Promenade" (*The Unforgettable Fire*); "Desire" (*Rattle and Hum*); "Even Better than the Real Thing," "Trying to Throw Your Arms Around the World" (*Achtung Baby*); "Zooropa," "The First Time" (*Zooropa*); "Staring at the Sun," "If You Wear That Velvet Dress" (*Pop*); "Wild Honey," "When I Look at the World" (*All That You Can't Leave Behind*); "All Because of You," "One Step Closer" (*How to Dismantle an Atomic Bomb*)
    Others?

4

PROPHECY AS JUDGMENT
AND HOPE

There's two kinds of people, there's those who are asleep
and those that are awake. I've used my music to wake me
up and if it wakes other people up on the way that's okay
because we get used to the sound of a bomb going off in
Belfast and to the roll call of bad news on television, we
get used to the fact that a third of the population on earth
are starving. We get used to all these things and we eventually fall asleep in the comfort of our freedom.

Bono

What Is Prophecy?

The Bible's books of prophecy are hard to read. They shake us
from slumber and force us to confront uncomfortable truths. For
many people God is a personal source of blessing and support, if
they believe at all. For many people, going to church and being

nice to others is the way to obey God. It is easy to see why, then, if you were coming from that sort of space, reading the prophets would be offensive. Rooted in the liberating leadership of Moses and stretching from Isaiah to Malachi, these fifteen passionate voices bring hope for blessing only after a considerable stripping down of our preconceived notions of God and God's expectations for humans. Take the opening of Isaiah as an example:

> Quit your worship charades.
>   I can't stand your trivial religious games:
> Monthly conferences, weekly Sabbaths, special meetings—
>   meetings, meetings, meetings—I can't stand one more!
> Meetings for this, meetings for that. I hate them!
>   You've worn me out!
> I'm sick of your religion, religion, religion,
>   while you go right on sinning.
> When you put on your next prayer-performance,
>   I'll be looking the other way.

Here is an attack on the status quo in the strongest terms. Bono's critique of churches as "bless-me clubs" finds its roots here in Isaiah.

What is at stake in such a full-on critique? What, indeed, when one considers the attack was aimed directly at the national duty to worship God at the temple? Simply the truth of biblical religion—God's people are called to be holy and to live lives that show forth holiness. Rather than turn a blind eye to a corrupt religious life that acts holy one day and defrauds the poor the next, Isaiah gives some cleanup advice:

> Sweep your lives clean of your evildoings
>   so I don't have to look at them any longer.
> Say no to wrong.
>   Learn to do good.

Work for justice.
　Help the down-and-out.
Stand up for the homeless.
　Go to bat for the defenseless. (1)

In so doing, the prophets argue, one finds true worship.

Old Testament scholar Walter Brueggemann argues that the prophets were concerned with the most elemental social change—the change in how people viewed the world. They understood the connection between public conviction and personal yearning. Most of all, they understood the distinctive power of language to speak in ways that evoke "a new thing." The prophetic task of evoking this "new thing" is the work of judgment of the present order and hope in evoking an alternative order.

Think back to the foundational event of Israel's life as a people—Moses, Aaron, and Miriam leading the people out of slavery in Egypt (Exodus 1–15). This story embodies both these elements: judgment and hope. First, the judgment of the present order begins with the divinely inspired capacity to grieve the suffering of God's people who had become slaves in Egypt. After an experience face to face with God in the desert, Moses returns to publicly lament that his people are in slavery. He brings the message from God, who said, "I've taken a good, long look at the affliction of my people in Egypt. I've heard their cries for deliverance from their slave masters; I know all about their pain. And now I have come down to help them, pry them loose from the grip of Egypt, and get them out of that country . . ." (Exodus 3). Such an announcement of grief names things that are not right, and breaks the sense of numbness that the overwhelming power of the status quo imposes on the people. When they heard of God's concern for their suffering, the people "bowed low and they worshiped" (Exodus 4).

The second half of the prophetic task follows when such grief is openly spoken and thereby opens a space for judgment and new hope. Those in power try to suppress open displays of grief, of naming injustice, in order to stifle the imagination of alternative realities. God tells Moses, continuing from the Exodus 3 quote above, ". . . and [I will] bring them to a good land with wide-open spaces, a land lush with milk and honey." The prophetic voice fights against the numbing power of dominant forces by evoking awareness, grief, and a vision of new life as God intends. Without the gift of imagination, no prophetic voice is possible. Thus prophecy is never simply denunciation; it always involves a sorrowful denunciation of the wrongs followed by a portrait of what is promised, the new thing God will do.

In Isaiah's time, hundreds of years after the Exodus and the establishment of the Israelite monarchy in the Promised Land, the people had managed to replicate the oppressive structures of Egypt. The kings of Israel had become worshippers of idols; the elite had been seduced by their privilege and come to depend on systematic oppression of the poor to maintain their palaces of cedar and ivory and gold. Isaiah, like the other biblical prophets, believed all the people had fallen away from faithfulness to God but held the leaders especially responsible. Isaiah presents this poetic image of the consequences to come:

> God enters the courtroom.
> > He takes his place at the bench to judge his people.
> God calls for order in the court,
> > hauls the leaders of his people into the dock:
> "You've played havoc with this country.
> > Your houses are stuffed with what you've stolen from the poor.
> What is this, anyway? Stomping on my people,
> > grinding the faces of the poor into the dirt? (Isaiah 3)

Isaiah's rhetorical flourish rises and falls through chapters of lament and grief and judgment. The core prophecy, Isaiah says, is that doom will befall "you who call evil good and good evil, who put darkness in place of light and light in place of darkness, who substitute bitter for sweet and sweet for bitter!" (Isaiah 5).

And indeed, doom does befall Jerusalem and its inhabitants. Isaiah predicted that the leaders would suppress his warnings and pay his judgments no heed. God told Isaiah to say: "Listen hard, but you aren't going to get it; Look hard, but you won't catch on" (Isaiah 6). And indeed, they did not, as Isaiah finally declares to King Hezekiah:

> I have to warn you, the time is coming when everything in this palace, along with everything your ancestors accumulated before you, will be hauled off to Babylon. God says that there will be nothing left. Nothing. And not only your things, but your *sons*. Some of your sons will be taken into exile, ending up as eunuchs in the palace of the king of Babylon. (Isaiah 39)

Isaiah and the prophets record the grief in the face of their predictions. "Tough men weep openly. Peacemaking diplomats are in bitter tears. The roads are empty—not a soul out on the streets" (Isaiah 33). They record the grief, but a new vision cannot come without going through the suffering to its bitter end.

Yet there, at the end, in the face of exile, humiliation, and suffering, the people are finally ready to hear a new vision, a fresh portrayal of God's invitation to new life. The prophet's poetic voice sings, painting a promised future that fills the imagination of the people in exile. Isaiah portrays the people saying, "I don't get it. God has left me. My master has forgotten I even exist." And then he speaks a word from the Lord,

"Can a mother forget the infant at her breast, walk away from the baby she bore? But even if mothers forget, I'd never forget you—never" (Isaiah 49). "This exile is just like the days of Noah for me: I promised then that the waters of Noah would never again flood the earth. I'm promising now no more anger, no more dressing you down" (Isaiah 54). Isaiah recalls both human and divine images that assure the people of God's promise and care.

Yet evoking hope does not stop with remembering a promise. It extends on to a vision of life made new. Here some of the most glorious passages of the Bible portray a vision of God's promised "shalom," a place where all things are made right.

> The Spirit of God, the Master, is on me
>   because God anointed me.
> He sent me to preach good news to the poor,
>   heal the heartbroken,
> Announce freedom to the captives,
>   pardon all prisoners.
> God sent me to announce the year of his grace. (Isaiah 61)

New priorities are established and set in the context of a whole new work of creation: "Pay close attention now: I'm creating new heavens and a new earth. All the earlier troubles, chaos, and pain are things of the past, to be forgotten. Look ahead with joy. Anticipate what I'm creating: I'll create Jerusalem as sheer joy, create my people as pure delight" (Isaiah 65).

Such powerful language offers a people made numb through suffering and led astray by idols a freedom to see themselves and the world in a whole new way. The freshness and energy that come from such proclamations turn us from despair and toward God's desire of abundant life for all. God's vision of equality in the new creation first comes as vision, as imagination, and as gift. From this gift of vision and spirit, we are drawn into the work of helping God to bring this about.

So often, the need for prophecy arises because we're not helping God. Rather, we've tried to either block God out or to force God to fit into our projects. The prophet's job is to say "You can't do that!" As Pastor Eugene Peterson says,

> If we won't face up, [prophets] grab us by the scruff of our necks and shake us into attention. Amos crafted poems, Jeremiah wept sermons, Isaiah alternately rebuked and comforted, Ezekiel did street theater. U2 writes songs and goes on tour, singing them.

I turn now to the task of showing some of the ways U2 fits into this litany of prophets.

The Howling Wind

U2 has been anxious at times not to wear their convictions on their sleeves where they are susceptible to media critique. After nearly a decade of writing and singing about the conflicts in Ireland, Central America, South Africa, and the United States, the *Rattle and Hum* double album and movie caught U2 in a riptide of fed-up critics. Their combination of preaching causes and their travel through American roots music garnered such accolades as "sincere egomania."

Famously pledging to "go away and dream it all up again" at their New Year's Eve concert at Dublin's Point Theater in 1989, U2 emerged in the 1990s in costume, using masks to make points they previously made in the most transparent of ways. As Journalist Bill Flanagan noted at the time, Bono drew inspiration from Oscar Wilde for this move: "Man is least himself when he talks in his own person; give him a mask and he will tell you the truth." Yet despite their efforts to deflect criticism by making their point indirectly (as the ZooTV tour did through the simulation of media overload on multiple video screens, each flashing contradicting messages), at times their charisma for direct appeals came crashing through.

On the 1997 tour titled PopMart, the typical set list included "Last Night On Earth" from the album *Pop*. Typically, Bono would introduce the song while the rhythm section began a chunky, haunted introduction:

> How did we get here, how did you get here? / I went looking, so much to see, I went looking. / I went looking for spirit, found alcohol. / Went looking for soul, and I bought some style. / I wanted to meet God, you sold me religion.

And as Bono shouts out the final line, the band comes in on the full groove of the song's melody.

While this might seem like a version of "The Wanderer" out tasting the fullness of the world (as I described in the previous chapter), this phrasing has an element of critique, of complaint, missing from Ecclesiastes' irenic mood. I'd have certainly missed it, but Beth Maynard, co-editor of a book of U2 sermons and a leader in the online conversations about U2 and religion, wrote:

> I've been studying Isaiah recently. . . . Isaiah is magnificent, but what I want to post about is the famous song of the vineyard in chapter 5. Its climax in verse 7 ("[God] looked for justice, but found bloodshed; for righteousness, but heard a cry") contains two well-known puns: "He looked for *mishpat*, but found *mispat*; for *tsedaqua*, but heard *tseaqua*." As I sat there thinking about that poetic device, the opening sound effects of the live versions of "Last Night On Earth" unexpectedly sounded in my head, and then I realized why: "I went looking for spirit,

but found alcohol / I went looking for soul, and I bought some style / I wanted to meet God, but you sold me religion."

This telling set of couplets introduces a song that embodies one key mode of prophecy in U2 songs: portraying the decadence and danger of a consumer culture where buying and seeking pleasure are elevated to the level of life or death.

The song "Last Night On Earth" tells the story of a woman lost in the fast life, burning the candle at both ends, and embracing its inevitable self-destruction. The opening verse combines her perspective—"She feels the ground is giving way / But she thinks we're better off that way"—with a somewhat tongue-in-cheek description of her perspective from an outsider—"The more you take, the less you feel / The less you know the more you believe / The more you have, the more it takes today." Then the chorus blows in with Bono singing at full volume, the Edge and Adam grinding away, and Larry focusing only on the cymbals for effect:

You gotta give it away / You gotta give it away / You gotta give it away / Give it away / You gotta give it away / You gotta give it away / Well she knows just what its worth / She's living like it's the last night on earth / The last night on earth.

The chorus, in the fine tradition of multifaceted U2 meanings, cuts at least two ways. But either seen as a goading to the woman to "go for it" as she parties all night or as a warning not to miss life's higher purpose of giving itself away in service to others rather that serving her own self-destructive pursuit of pleasure, the power of the song is disturbing. Indeed, the remix version, released as a b-side on the single, is subtitled "First Night in Hell Mix."

The song "Numb," from the album *Zooropa*, might go even further in its embodiment of their "new" approach that imagines prophecy as art, offering a portrait of what is wrong in society. "Numb," a lyric written by the Edge during the *Achtung Baby* sessions in Berlin, offers an utterly overwhelming litany of "Don't"s, sung as well by the Edge, and joined toward the latter part of the song by a falsetto chorus (sung by Bono) and a simple loop that proclaims: "I feel numb" (sung by Larry).

> Don't move / Don't talk out-a time / Don't think / Don't worry / everything's just fine / Just fine / Don't grab / Don't clutch / Don't hope for too much / Don't breathe / Don't achieve / Don't grieve without leave / Don't check, just balance on the fence / Don't answer / Don't ask / Don't try and make sense.

Bono says of the song, "we're trying to recreate the feeling of sensory overload." In a certain sense, U2's emphasis—in songs and in live concerts—was to become more intentionally focused on art. The effort, rooted in their reading of cultural theorists such as Jean Baudrillard and theologians such as C. S. Lewis, took the form of prophetic portrayal of the dangers and contradictions of postmodern life in Europe and North America.

To call "Last Night On Earth" and "Numb" the voice of prophecy connects those songs to a whole ethos of U2's work in the 1990s that they, at certain points, playfully called "judo." Bono, at the end of three years of touring with ZooTV in support of the albums *Achtung Baby* and *Zooropa*, said he did think they'd achieved their goal "to describe the age and challenge it."

> We were confirmed about our instincts that the idea of counterculture, the way it used to be in the sixties, that number is up. And I'm interested in these more Asian ideas, which we playfully call judo, that you use the energy of what's going

against you—and by that I just mean popular culture, commerce, science—to defend yourself. Rather than resistance, in the hippie or punk sense of the world, you try to walk through it rather than walk away from it. As opposed to the old ideas of dropping out and forming your own Garden of Eden—the sort of brown-rice position.

After the way their idealism was lampooned in the late1980s, U2 found a new way to speak their values. As Bono put it, "If people today see you coming with a placard these days they just get out of your way. U2 has got to be careful. And smart." Smart meant a modulation of their use of the prophetic voice—one that let them survive and go forward in the context of the excesses of the 1990s.

Yet for this 1990s prophetic mode to make sense I need to return to their early exploration of the prophetic voice—when they carried a placard for their concerns, so to speak—especially as it took shape on the albums *War* and *The Joshua Tree*. Here, they first began to exercise a bold and explicit voice that mirrors the shape of a prophetic voice described above. I have already described the opening song on the album *War*, "Sunday Bloody Sunday," as echoing the shape of the psalms. Yet in this context, the song shows all the elements of the prophetic voice: grief (I can't believe the news today / I can't close my eyes and make it go away) followed by critique (And the battle's just begun / There's many lost, but tell me who has won?) that gives way to a vision of hope and a new reality ('Cos tonight / We can be as one, tonight / Wipe the tears from your eyes / Wipe your tears away).

The theme of *War*, which was decidedly anti-war, continued in "Seconds," the second song on the album that, according to Bono, has been unfairly ignored. This song, more than the other more earnest songs on *War*, prefigures their use of irony as a part of their prophetic voice. With lead singing and

67

key ideas from the Edge, the song begins with a driving drum and bass line accompanied by a jangley acoustic guitar. Soon, Edge's voice comes in with what is by any account a clearly ambiguous lyric: "Takes a second to say goodbye, say goodbye / Takes a second to say goodbye, say goodbye." It is not until a full two minutes into the song that one begins to clue into the meaning. In the middle of the song, they sample from a 1982 TV documentary titled "Soldier Girls." Edge comments:

> The whole spectacle of these girls going through this incredible routine of training seemed perfect to slip in here in the middle. It's not obvious but if you listen close you can hear the refrain "I want to be an airborne ranger / I want to live a life of danger." It's very disturbing.

And then the songs lyric becomes clear as day: "Push the button and pull the plug / Say goodbye, oh, oh, oh" and then "And they're doing the atomic bomb / Do they know where the dance comes from?" The band did know and, as Bono commented at the time: "I've always felt ill at the concept of nuclear fall-out. We are the first generation of people to have to live with that possibility." And it is something that has followed the band, influencing the title of two future albums (*The Unforgettable Fire*, a reference to the bombing of Hiroshima, and *How to Dismantle an Atomic Bomb*).

While *War's* emphasis was on the "Troubles" in Ireland, their next two albums, especially *The Joshua Tree*, take a more explicit look at the United States—the good and the bad. Whereas *War* spoke in unmistakable terms about the problems of violence and war, as well as sectarian violence in their homeland, *The Joshua Tree* picks up themes of unease about American power in the world at the same time as the band was receiving tremendous support from America. Still, through the mid-1980s they had been involved in various projects that were a crash course in social justice. This led to their desire for *The Joshua Tree* and the tour that followed to serve as a wake-up call to the U.S. As Bono put it,

> It's not your first reason for being on stage, to effect change in the political climate of a country. I don't know what the first reason is, but that's not the first reason. But I'd like to think that U2 have already contributed to a turnaround in thinking.

Such political awareness had been building through the mid-1980s—through an immersion in Martin Luther King Jr.'s philosophy of nonviolence, through playing a famine relief concert called "Live Aid," and a subsequent summer trip to Africa working among refugees (see chapter 5), and a visit to Central America with people they met at a church in San Francisco called Glide Memorial.

It was the trip to Nicaragua and El Salvador that led to what may be U2's most severe prophetic impulse. This prophetic impulse bears all the anger of Isaiah 3 when he shouts "What is this, anyway? Stomping on my people / Grinding the faces of the poor into the dirt?" Captured in a few powerful songs on *The Joshua Tree*, this passion is most clearly exemplified in "Bullet the Blue Sky," a searing portrayal of the result of American foreign policy in Central America that has been a concert staple ever since. The subsequent tour supporting *The Joshua Tree*, and the double CD and movie that followed, all bore the title *Rattle and Hum*, a phrase taken from this song. When they began the song on that tour in outdoor stadium venues, a large American flag in a fireworks panel would light up while the speakers wailed out a sample of Jimi Hendrix's version of "The Star Spangled Banner." As the fireworks begin to fade out, the insistent drum and base line break in with a rising line of guitar on one single note until all of a sudden the guitar breaks off into a shooting downward tone, followed by another, followed by another.

69

Bono's voice comes in, adding gritty words to make clear the musical picture being painted by the band:

> In the howling wind / Comes a stinging rain / See them driving nails / Into souls on the tree of pain / From the firefly / a red orange glow / I see the face of fear / Running scared in the valley below.

Bono recalls his experience in El Salvador:

> There was a kind of ethnic cleansing with a government health warning. They would tell the people: "Get out of your villages, we're about to bomb the s**t out of you." Military sponsored by the Land of the Free, terrorizing peasant farmers. It was unbelievable. Because people wouldn't have left their villages; they were in their homes. It was carnage. It was awful. It was the other side of America. It's along time ago now, but in order to remember it, I tried to turn it into music, in the song "Bullet the Blue Sky."

While originally aimed at waking up America to the duplicity of speaking freedom out of one side of its mouth and horror out of the other side, the song has come to be a multipurpose critique of the ways nations and peoples can value ideas over people.

While on the ZooTV tour in the mid-1990s, U2 played at the Olympic Stadium Hitler built as a monument to German greatness. In previous shows during this tour "Bullet the Blue Sky" had been accompanied by blood red lighting, and then, at the right moment in the song, flaming crosses filled the multiple giant video screens. The images echo the lines of the song: "You plant a demon seed / You raise a flower of fire / We see them burning crosses / see the flames, higher and higher." But in Germany, where the display of the swastika is illegal,

the video display of burning crosses morphed sideways to become flaming swastikas, and Bono shouted, *"Dieses geschieht
nie wieder!"* (This will never happen again!) Such shouts take
on the voice of prophecy, not in some sense of knowing the
future, but in the sense of portraying grief-filled anger at what
has been in order to make space for other visions. The fans
that night responded with wild cheers.

After ending their trilogy of albums in the 1990s with the
somber lament "Wake Up, Dead Man," their first song on the
first album of the new millennium strikes a remarkably hopeful note. Titled "Beautiful Day," the tune begins with what
seems to be an unmistakable heartbeat base drum rhythm,
accompanied by chiming guitar, and soon a shaking tambourine. To someone familiar with gospel music in church, it has
an obvious gospel quality. Producer Daniel Lanois remarked,
"It's like a hymn—I believe the song has that in its backbone."
And indeed, when Bono begins to sing, the music again fore-
shadows the tone: "The heart is a bloom, shoots up through
stony ground." Suffering has not been avoided on the way to
hope; the heart blooms from a shoot in the stony ground.

"Beautiful Day" picked up on the vibe of the band—and
especially Bono—after years of working on the Jubilee 2000
campaign. Started by religious groups who wanted to see the
year 2000 amount to more than fireworks and parties, the campaign sought to influence governments and banks to forgive
crippling debts held by many of the world's poorest nations.
When Bono was asked in the late 1990s to be a spokesman
for this effort, he didn't realize the extent to which his celebrity would open doors. But by the end of the campaign, and
after meeting such diverse figures as the pope (with whom
he famously traded blue sunglasses for a rosary) and arch-
conservative United States Senator Jesse Helms (who reportedly cried as Bono retold stories of children dying of AIDS

71

in Africa), Bono had a new respect for the admittedly absurd power he could employ for good. While in the 1980s he had helped raise 200 million dollars for famine relief through the Live Aid experience, the Jubilee 2000 campaign succeeded in commitments to reduce the total third world debt by one third, or about 100 billion dollars.

"Beautiful Day" opens up a vision of hope for a new heaven and a new earth. It struggles with the real feelings of despair someone who has seen suffering knows to be true: "The traffic is stuck and you're not moving anywhere / You thought you'd found a friend to take you out of this place." But this stuckness does not win the day; the prophet also speaks a word of the new vision God promises and that we, like Noah, are given the task of helping to secure. Evoking the end of the flood story in Genesis, when after forty days and forty nights in the ark, Noah sends out a dove to find a sign of dry land, Bono sings: "See the bird with a leaf in her mouth / After the flood all the colors came out." After the flood, God gave the rainbow in the sky as a sign of the promise never to destroy the earth again. Bono continues, "It was a beautiful day / Don't let it get away / Beautiful day / Touch me, take me to that other place / Teach me, I know I'm not a hopeless case."

In part because of this buoyant spirit on their new album, titled *All That You Can't Leave Behind,* U2 connected with the deeply wounded spirit of the United States after the attacks of September 11, 2001. Their third leg of the Elevation tour began in Madison Square Garden not long after that fateful September day, and during that and subsequent concerts, they scrolled the names of those who had died on the huge projection screens behind them. Asked to do the halftime of the Super Bowl that following January, U2 included a version of "Beautiful Day." Somehow, in the midst of evil we cannot explain, we still long for and claim God's promise of a new day.

Bono, singing at full voice, turned his face skywards, reaching his hand upwards as he sings to God before hundreds of millions watching world-wide, "Touch me, take me to that other place / Teach me, I know I'm not a hopeless case." The prophetic voice, moving through sorrowful judgment, to be sure, but in the face of destruction and unbelievable suffering, speaking also the tender and powerful vision of hope and a new day.

Additional U2 Songs Echoing the Voice of the Prophets

"October" (*October*); "New Year's Day" (*War*); "Pride—In the Name of Love" (*The Unforgettable Fire*); "Red Hill Mining Town"; "In God's Country" (*The Joshua Tree*); "Silver and Gold" (*Rattle and Hum*); "Zoo Station" (*Achtung Baby*); "Please" (*Pop*); "Walk On" (*All That You Can't Leave Behind*); "Love and Peace or Else" (*How to Dismantle an Atomic Bomb*)

Others?

5

PARABLES AS OFFENSE AND MERCY

Jesus declared that His parables were not to make the
meaning easy but inaccessible to the idly curious who
"having ears, do not hear . . ."

Bono

What Are Parables?

Parables are hard to understand on purpose. They often
confuse the listener, especially in their briefest form. Parables
are also dangerous. They are intentionally deceptive, distract-
ing and dislocating to those who listen. They often offend
proper sensibilities. The offense may be misunderstood, or if
understood, either lead to angry rejection of the implications,
or the breaking open of new possibilities.

Take one of Jesus's most famous parables as an example.
In the Gospel of Luke, chapter 13, Jesus is in the synagogue
teaching those gathered. He says:

What is the kingdom of God like? And to what can I compare it? It is like a grain of mustard seed that a man took and sowed in his garden; and it grew and became a tree, and the birds of the air made nests in its branches. (NRSV)

In the modern West, this text is often heard as a prediction that the movement Jesus initiates begins modestly but grows immeasurably over time. So, as the simple moral lesson goes, don't discount what seems to be modest in its beginnings. Have faith! But in context, this story is a calculated offense in order to turn people from their own desires toward God's desire for them.

To see the offense, the satire within the parable of the mustard seed, one has to understand that parables are intended to be an offense, and then seek out clues to what that intention might have been. So when we ask what scriptural references might have been in people's minds, we're going in the right direction. In Ezekiel 31, the Pharaoh of Egypt is likened to a cedar in Lebanon, with its top in the clouds and with long branches, where birds of the air make their nests. In chapter 4, the prophet Daniel uses this exact same figure in describing the Babylonian king Nebuchadnezzar. And in Ezekiel 17 and elsewhere this same powerful imperial image is projected onto the coming Messiah and his kingdom. Rather than embrace this image of the mighty empires of the world, with the implication that he will lead a revolt against the Roman occupation currently ruling his land, Jesus offers a reversal aimed at offending the congregation's sensibilities and opening space for a new understanding of God's kingdom to emerge. You can imagine the whispering in the back of the crowd: "A mustard seed! The smallest of seeds and from it grows a shrub-tree, if you can even call it a tree—round and gangly! *That* is the image he gives of the kingdom?"

76

Jesus knew that many would not understand. He even found that his own disciples did not understand fully until after his death and resurrection. He predicted this, drawing on the words of his prophetic forbearer, Isaiah, after a parable about planting seeds. Talking to the disciples, Jesus said:

> You've been given insight into God's kingdom — you know how it works. But to those who can't see it yet, everything comes in stories, creating readiness, nudging them toward receptive insight. These are people —
>
> > Whose eyes are open but don't see a thing,
> > Whose ears are open but don't understand a word,
> > Who avoid making an about-face and getting forgiven.
> > (Mark 4)

Jesus understood the intense conflict of his situation, and he knew that he had to speak truth in ways that both criticized so as to open space for God to work and protected him from those who would destroy him in order to protect their own positions of power and prestige. Jesus's use of the Isaiah tradition reaches even farther back in tradition, grounded in the belief that God sometimes "hardens the hearts" of political opponents, as Yahweh did with Pharaoh (Exodus 7). He knew what was going to happen to him, and he believed that it was "necessary" that these opponents — the scribes and Pharisees — did not see and understand. Then, God's full plan for salvation would come to pass and many indeed would see, and hear, turn, and find forgiveness.

In order to give guidance to those who would see, hear, turn, and find forgiveness, Jesus spoke many parables that give concrete shape to the life of one who loves God. These parables, often told in brief and provocative form, likely offended them as much as Jesus's general redefinition of the idea of Messiah and God's coming kingdom. One of the most famous parables, the so-called parable of the prodigal son, is recounted in Luke's Gospel, chapter 15. In this chapter, Jesus tells a series of stories about finding things that are lost—a sheep, a coin, a son—all framed by an introductory comment by Luke. He writes:

> By this time a lot of men and women of doubtful reputation were hanging around Jesus, listening intently. The Pharisees and religion scholars were not pleased, not at all pleased. They growled, "He takes in sinners and eats meals with them, treating them like old friends."

Parables work, as I said above, because they play off of the expectations of the hearers. Those listening have every reason to expect the one outcome set up by the story's beginning, but then the opposite conclusion comes to pass and the hearer's expectations are turned on their head.

In the case of the parable of the prodigal (or lost) son, Jesus describes a man who is the head of a large household. One of his two sons comes to ask his father for his inheritance—what he would rightfully expect upon his father's death. His father agrees to give it to him, and the younger son makes off with the cash to party in a far away city. He wastes it all and finds himself impoverished, feeding slop to pigs and wondering if his father would take him back. While he has no right to return as family, having renounced his father as dead and piddled away all of his inheritance, he hopes he might be allowed back as a servant. Meanwhile, the elder son has remained faithful, working with his father.

At this point in the parable, listeners are on the edge of their seats, waiting for the other shoe to drop when the insolent younger son returns and gets an earful and a boot in the pants from his angry father. They are ready to have a laugh at his expense and to have their values reaffirmed about family and loyalty. But just here, the parable does its offensive work. Luke picks up with the younger son on the road home:

> When he was still a long way off, his father saw him. His heart pounding, he ran out, embraced him, and kissed him. The son started his speech: "Father, I've sinned against God, I've sinned before you; I don't deserve to be called your son ever again."
>
> But the father wasn't listening. He was calling to the servants, "Quick. Bring a clean set of clothes and dress him. Put the family ring on his finger and sandals on his feet. Then get a grain-fed heifer and roast it. We're going to a feast! We're going to have a wonderful time! My son is here—given up for dead and now alive! Given up for lost and now found!"

The hearers begin to murmur among themselves, and Luke cleverly weaves their responses into the voice of the older son: "Outrageous! This 'son' wasted his money on whores and fine wine, and you throw a big party. I've been faithful for all these years and you've never done the same for me!" Outrageous. That is the image we're left with of God. That is the vision we're left with as a way of life for those who love God.

It is worth noting who is most offended by Jesus's parables. It is the ultra-righteous believers and the religious scholars who, at the beginning of Luke's chapter, stand together murmuring. And just a short while later in the story, Luke records that "the high priests, religion scholars, and leaders of the people were trying their best to find a way to get rid of him" (Luke 19). It is no surprise, then, to learn that some of U2's most effective use of the parable form in their songs garnered the strongest negative reaction from the ultra-righteous believers and leaders of the people. They have, to their credit, gone ahead anyway, even though it has meant that they have been maligned and misunderstood. While some have misunderstood, others have taken the offense to heart, finding that in the midst of being off balance, God finds a way to move and warm their hearts toward a deeper and more profound connection to the kingdom coming (on earth, as it is in Heaven).

Waiting on Crumbs

U2 has from early on felt that their art was in and of itself a reflection of God's gift and blessing on the band. Through the spirit-filled renewal at Mount Temple, their high school in Dublin, and in the years just after high school in an intense Christian community, the band has developed a sense of their music and art as a holy gift (though, I should note, Adam was agnostic regarding these faith commitments at the time. He has since become a Christian and Bono describes him as "the most spiritually centered of the band"). Yet they also felt that as art, their music ought to be free from formulas that bind Christian artists to narrow confessional limits. U2, it seems, found singing in parables *necessary* because it is a genre that paints pictures and points to something without saying it directly.

Why are parables necessary? Bono, reflecting on the band's early realization about the power of their spirit-driven style of rock and roll, said:

> There was a moment where myself and Edge sat around . . . and we came to the realization: "Hold on a second. Where are these gifts coming from? This is how we worship God, even though we don't write religious songs, because we didn't feel God needs the advertising."

Well, on occasion U2 has written and sung "religious songs" (even sampling "Amazing Grace" in concerts). On the whole, however, the band has struggled to find the fullest means to live out of the gifts they've been given. This has meant that U2 has struggled to be a great rock and roll band in ways that evoke a Christian ethos without being obviously Christian. They have managed to write songs that are personally moving as well as socially relevant. And they increasingly write songs that explore the full register of religious experience, believing that in the search for God no place is totally forsaken. Two examples of songs sung in the parabolic mode exemplify how they seek to make space to unsettle those who are too comfortable in their certainty about who God is and what God asks of us.

"The First Time," from the mid-1990's album *Zooropa*, shows how the parable form helped U2 to explore the search for God in the midst of the world's confusion. On this track, a mournful gospel-sounding vocal moves through a trinity of verses, each time followed by the line, "but for the first time I feel love." In the first, Bono describes having " a lover like no other/ she got soul, soul, soul, sweet soul/ and she teach me how to sing/ Shows me colors when there's none to see/ gives me hope when I can't believe." After understanding Bono's attraction to wisdom literature and the feminine imagery for God, it is easy to see here the reference is the Holy Spirit. In the second verse, he describes having a brother when he is in need, "I spend my whole time running / He spends his running after me." Here is Christ the redeemer, the seeker of the lost coin, the shepherd who looks for the lost sheep (Luke 15). In the third verse, he meets a rich man who gives him "the keys to his kingdom (coming)." The rich man is understood to be God the Father as portrayed by Jesus (Luke 15). The song has the rich man say "I have many mansions / and there are many rooms to see." But, Bono sings, "I left through the back door / And I threw away the key."

81

The song has obvious connections to Jesus's parables in the Bible, but it is itself a parable in form. The obvious meaning, for the ultra-religious person, would be that of the prodigal son returning. The Spirit gives him hope when he can't believe, the Son rescues him when he feels himself going down, and upon his return, the Father gives him a royal welcome—the keys to the kingdom and a cup of gold. Of course, the prodigal who has found his way home ought to rejoice and find rest in the welcome. But he does not. He doesn't want it, and he goes off wandering again. He throws away the keys. The song is a parable of losing faith, something that strikes the ultra-religious as a sure ticket to damnation. Bono is not so sure, and here he tries on that feeling through this alternative ending to the well-known tale. It is not his own story, as he says: "It's about losing your faith. I haven't lost my faith. I've a great deal of faith. But that song expresses a moment a lot of people feel." Perhaps, then, his empathy opens up space for those who have experienced this loss to see again how a lover, a brother, or a father might be seeking them still.

A second song that embodies the mode of parables focuses less on personal faith and more on the church's inaction. The song "Crumbs from Your Table" steps hard on the toes of the ultra-religious, especially in the United States. In an interview, Bono said, "I went to speak to Christian fundamentalist groups in America to convince them to give money to fight AIDS in Africa. It was like getting blood from a stone. I told them about a hospice in Uganda where so many people were dying they had to sleep three to a bed. Sister Ann, who I mention in the song, works at that hospice."

"Crumbs from Your Table" is one of the songs on 2004's album *How To Dismantle An Atomic Bomb*, and it clearly comes out of the activism Bono and the band have taken on in especially dramatic ways since the Jubilee 2000 campaign.

Bono, well aware now of how easily he can be targeted for living as an ultra-rich rock star while advocating for the poorest of the poor, says "I see my role as raising the alarm. I have a very loud hailer. My bullhorn is plugged into a Marshall stack, and I can use this ridiculous thing called celebrity to the advantage of these things."

Some people imagine "Crumbs from Your Table" takes its lead from the parable of the Canaanite woman in Matthew's Gospel, chapter 15, where there is a story of a woman whose daughter is possessed and who wants Jesus's help. When he hears of her request, he responds by saying he has come for "the lost sheep of Israel," and "it is not right to take bread out of children's mouths and throw it to dogs." Jesus's attention to his own people (the lost sheep of Israel) is the expected response. But the outcome ends up quite different. The woman is feisty and does not stand for this dismissal. She retorts: "Even the dogs eat the crumbs from the master's table!" (NIV) Jesus relents and says, "Oh, woman, your faith is something else!" The image of this persistent and feisty woman fits the image U2 projects of Africa as beautiful and proud, ready to work for their own improvement if the playing field were only level (as the band so vividly illustrates in the hand-drawing from the book accompanying *How To Dismantle An Atomic Bomb* in the deluxe edition—it is a soccer field with one end elevated!)

Another relevant parable with the line "crumbs from the table" is the parable of the rich man and Lazarus from Luke's Gospel. There, Jesus tells the story of a rich man, always dressed in fine clothing and enjoying life. At his gate, a poor man lay covered with sores, begging for the crumbs that fall from the rich man's table. Again, putting the parable theory of reversal into play, it would have been typical in that day to see the rich man as blessed by God and the man covered

83

with sores as under God's judgment. Yet, the parable goes on to say, when they both died the beggar was taken up into heaven, while the rich man went to hell. This would have offended the hearers who assumed that while the rich man might owe charity to the poor man to keep him from starving, he certainly would not seek to interact with him, or more than that, try to rehabilitate him. The beggar was at best an unclean sinner who deserved his suffering and was to be avoided at all costs by those who are righteous for fear they, too, would be tainted.

The song assumes rightly that many in America believe themselves to be—like the rich man in the parable—"special" in God's eyes, and our prosperity to be divinely ordained given our "special" place. Yet from the first couplet, U2 calls such an interpretation into question: "From the brightest star / Comes the blackest hole." Commenting on the legacy of colonialism and exploitation of Africa for slaves and raw materials verses the paltry amount of foreign aid offered to the poorest nations, Bono sings, "I was there for you baby / When you needed my help / Would you deny for others / What you demand for yourself?" And then as if anger overtakes the band at this point, Bono shifts into a two line refrain "Cool down, mama, cool off / Cool down mama, cool off" before being able to sing the chorus: "You speak of signs and wonders / I need something other / I would believe if I was able / But I'm waiting on the crumbs from your table."

It is important to note that in the parable, and in the song, there is no condemnation of money, or having a lot of it, but there is certainly a question of what qualifies as a righteous use of money. If we believe, as U2 does, that what we have is a surprising and unmerited gift from God, then what we have ought to serve more than our own needs. If this is true, then it makes more sense to say, as the song does in verse three, "Where you live should not decide / Whether you live or whether you die." Just prior to this parable in Luke 16, Jesus comments "No workers can serve two bosses; He'll either hate the first and love the second or adore the first and despise the second. You can't serve both God and the Bank." Luke then continues with commentary: "When the Pharisees, a money-loving bunch, heard him say these things, they rolled their eyes, dismissing him as hopelessly out of touch."

Bono has been accused of the same, but he keeps on script in his rounds of speeches at Ivy League graduations, political speeches, and television appearances. On one typical recent occasion, addressing the Labour Party Annual Conference, Bono recalled his 1984 summer trip to Wello, Ethiopia with his wife, Alison Stewart.

> We lived there for six weeks, working in an orphanage. On our last day at the orphanage a man handed me his baby and said, "take him with you." He knew in Ireland his son would live; in Ethiopia his son would die. I turned him down. In that moment I started this journey.

Later in the speech, though, he turns from Africa to Europe and America:

> Earlier I described the deaths of 6500 Africans a day from preventable, treatable diseases like AIDS: I watched people queuing up to die, three in a bed, in Malawi. That's Africa's crisis. But the fact that we in Europe or America are not treating it like an emergency—and the fact that its not every day on the news, well that is our crisis. And that's not horses**t, that's something much worse, I don't even know what that says about us.

The song "Crumbs from Your Table" concludes with similar sentiments: "Three to a bed / Sister Ann, she said / Dignity passes by."

The parable in Luke 16 concludes with the rich man in hell, begging Abraham to let him return to warn his five brothers so that they will change and avoid his awful fate. Abraham denied the request, however, saying, "They have Moses and the Prophets to tell them the score. Let them listen to them." Perhaps, just perhaps, God is using this rock star singer to point us back to the parables, to the prophets, and to Moses, so that we can rise to the moment and escape the hell on earth that so many people live in today. And by using globalization to redefine the reach of this parable, Bono remarks: "There was this old definition of generosity, which is at the very least the rich man looks after the poor man on his street. Guess what? Now, that street goes round the world."

U2 speaks in parables, in part, because they are deeply grounded in the world of scripture. It is how they think, how they see the world, how they understand what matters most in the world. Despite themselves, echoes of parables come out in their speech and song. Yet they also know the usefulness of speaking purposefully in parables. Art is at its worst when it is simple and transparent. Art stretches us, questions us, and leads us into new worlds. And expecting U2 to toss aside their art for faith presented in a simple for-mula not only misses the power of their art to help us clear space to see God and the world anew, it also misses the fact that much of the Bible is poetry and parable, artistic writing forms, and at times altogether challenging. Truth comes in many forms; one gift of U2 is showing how varied faithful truth seeking can be.

Additional U2 Songs Echoing Parables

"I Fall Down" (*October*); "Trip Through Your Wires" (*The Joshua Tree*); "The First Time" (*Zooropa*); "Playboy Mansion" (*Pop*); "Miracle Drug," "Crumbs from Your Table" (*How to Dismantle an Atomic Bomb*)

Others?

6

APOCALYPSE AS ECSTASY
AND HEALING

Sometimes people go to a concert, any concert, and they're nervous. There's tension there and, at some concerts I've been to, the tension is still there at the end when people walk out. A U2 concert seems to be different, and that's the healing thing, the washing thing. I really believe that rock 'n' roll is very powerful.

Bono, 1984

If you see us in front of 100,000 people, and you ask, do you want to go on a journey to somewhere that none of us have ever been before, to that place where you forget yourself, and who you are, and where you can imagine something better? It's a spine-chilling moment for you as a singer and for anyone in the audience.

Bono, 2001

89

What Is Apocalyse?

Typically, when people have an association with the term "apocalypse" it is from the tradition of end-times prophecy featured in such books as the best-selling *Left Behind* series. Google the term and the same type of associations come up: visions of the anti-Christ, fire, and the destruction of the world, while saints float off into the clouds with a glowing Jesus. Defining the term helps broaden this admittedly hyped understanding: apocalyptic visions are a "disclosure of heavenly secrets in visionary forms to a seer for the benefit of a religious community experiencing suffering or perceiving itself as victimized by some form of deprivation."

Apocalypse, taken from the Greek word *apokalyptein*, to reveal, is therefore used as a way to describe a vision of a better place. Typically, this means that the vision portrays some resolution to the present circumstances, either alleviation of suffering or rescue from oppression and victimization. The visions, often heavenly or at least envisioning a time beyond current suffering, have much in common with the prophetic visions, as this example from Isaiah shows: "Pay close attention now: I'm creating new heavens and a new earth. All the earlier troubles, chaos, and pain are things of the past, to be forgotten. Look ahead with joy" (Isaiah 65).

While biblical examples of apocalyptic writing generally share this common definition, they differ in the sorts of alienation or crises addressed. So while the method of response is similar, the details vary accordingly. One major biblical vision found in the book of Daniel provides support for people who are under persecution, a circumstance shared by the Gospel of Mark (not surprisingly, Mark quotes Daniel more than any other Old Testament book). Here, then, I'd like to look back at one chapter from Daniel and then pick up how that portion of Daniel is used in Mark.

Daniel is a book composed of stories and visions of obedience in a time and place hostile to following God. While the book was likely written at the time of the Persian occupation of Israel, its setting is in exile in Babylon. Chapter 7 is the first vision, following up on six stories (including the famous story of Daniel in the lion's den in chapter 6). The vision begins with Daniel asleep. In his dream, he looks and sees four winds whipping up a great storm on the ocean as four huge animals, each different from each other, emerge from the sea. The beasts are bizarre and fierce, including a lion with wings of an eagle, a bear that is told to "attack, devour, fill your belly," a panther with four heads, and the last a grisly horror with iron teeth to crunch and swallow its victims.

These four grotesque monsters represent hundreds of years of oppression and suffering for God's people. At this point in Daniel's narrative, a dramatic shift of scene takes place, now moving from the foaming sea to the calm of a courtroom. Daniel writes, "As I was watching all this,

> Thrones were set in place
> and The Old One sat down
> His robes were white as snow,
> his hair was white like wool.

All four of the monsters are subdued and die having "no power to rule." And Daniel sees a new person coming into the room:

> I saw a human form, a son of man,
> arriving in a whirl of clouds.
> He came to The Old One
> snd was presented to him.
> He was given power to rule—all the glory of royalty.

91

Daniel asks a bystander for an interpretation and learns that although four kingdoms will appear on earth, eventually the holy people of God will be given the kingdom and have it forever. It is a bold vision that can look almost five hundred years of oppression and dislocation in the face and declare that the God of heaven and earth is alone the true reality worthy of worship.

The time of Jesus was not, however, a time when the holy people were given the kingdom, but rather the time of the repression of a fifth occupier in their land—the Romans. There were numerous points of great social unrest during this time, and other writings like that of Daniel were written to inspire the people to hope beyond the suffering of the present. Jesus surely grew up with these stories and knew of other Jewish rebel leaders who some thought to be the Messiah but who were often killed in moments of violent uprising. These rebels thought they knew God's time and were attempting to force the vision of God's rule into existence by their own violent force.

Jesus, however, had another sort of apocalyptic understanding of leadership rooted in transformative suffering love. Like Daniel, Mark portrays the suffering of the people and bids them to face it with trust in the power of God rather than their own power. Jesus's invitation to a politics of nonviolent resistance shows the only real way to faithfulness to God and this-worldly transformation of the powers set against God's people. Take the Gospel of Mark, chapter 8, for instance, in the famous passage where one of the core disciples, Peter, has just correctly identified Jesus as "the Christ, the Messiah." At this point, Jesus explains that he will suffer, be tried by the leaders, die, and after three days rise again. But given the general climate of Palestine, Peter's protest to this vision shows they were rather ready to get weapons and follow their Messiah into battle against the hated Romans and their Jewish puppet government led by Herod.

Jesus strongly rebukes Peter and announces that instead of leading his disciples off into bloody guerilla warfare, he wants his followers to embrace suffering. Jesus calls to the crowd to join the disciples and says,

> Anyone who intends to come with me has to let me lead. You're not in the driver's seat; *I* am. Don't run from suffering; embrace it. Follow me and I'll show you how. Self-help is no help at all. Self-sacrifice is the way, my way, to saving yourself, your true self. What good would it do to get everything you want and lose you, the real you? What could you ever trade your soul for?

This must have come as a shock, for when Jesus says the word "suffering," the Greek word is *stauron*, cross, raising the specter of Roman power. They were well known for their methods of exerting control by taking rebels and criminals and hanging them from crosses in the most public places—town squares or on hills just outside the city gate. What could Jesus possibly mean here?

And in a remarkable move that evokes Daniel's vision in the courtroom where the Old One passes judgment and the Son of Man is given authority over all things, Jesus tells the disciples and crowds:

> "If any of you are embarrassed over me and the way I'm leading you when you get around your fickle and unfocused friends, know that you'll be an even greater embarrassment to the Son of Man when he arrives in all the splendor of God, his Father, with an army of the holy angels." Then he drove it home by saying, "This isn't pie in the sky by and by. Some of you who

are standing here are going to see it happen, see the kingdom of God arrive in full force."

Here, like Daniel, Jesus portrays the reality of God's ultimate authority and the necessity of following his way of active, suffering love that alone will transform the world into God's vision and likeness. Those disciples must choose (and the moment of choice comes for all disciples) if they will stand with Jesus, taking up their cross, or if they will continue to seek violent means to seek the peace and freedom of the people.

The portrayal of Jesus's death on the cross and his call to disciples to also take up their cross and follow initially seems to be failure. The promise of the movement of God in this man Jesus seems to be lost in the teeth of the Roman monster. Yet the vision of Mark and Daniel clearly shows the judgment of Almighty God bringing Jesus from the grip of death to Easter's resurrection and the movement Jesus began from chaos to clarity of spirit on Pentecost. To those in the midst of confusion and doubt, suffering under persecution and hostility, such a vision — of a powerful promise of ultimate victory and courage within the struggle from day to day — offers the sustenance for maintaining faithfulness. Such courage to remain faithful was needed by Daniel in the Babylonian exile, by Jesus's friends under Roman occupation, and by many throughout the history of the church in various kinds of situations, from the Roman persecution of the early church to the civil rights movement in the United States and many more.

Apocalyptic writings offer more than a vision of God's ultimate victory that lends courage to the suffering faithful. These writings also offer some of the most beautiful visions of what that day will look like when God's rule is established on earth. The last book in the Bible, Revelation (also know by its other title, the Apocalypse of John) was written during a difficult time in the life of the early church. The Roman Empire worshipped Caesar as Lord and held many local gods as worthy of worship and sacrifice. They were hostile to the church and repressed it in many places over hundreds of years. And in the midst of this, perhaps even from a prison island, John wrote beautiful poetic visions of the earth renewed by God's power, restored according to God's vision and judgment.

These apocalyptic visions of creation restored have their roots in the prophetic visions of the end of exile, of a renewed life beyond the destruction of Israel. I quoted Isaiah's vision of "new heavens and a new earth" above. In that vision, Isaiah sees a new Jerusalem that is God's "sheer joy" and "pure delight." There are "no more sounds of weeping in the city, no cries of anguish; no more babies dying in the cradle, or old people who don't enjoy a full lifetime." In announcing this new city, Isaiah 60 proclaims, "Get out of bed, Jerusalem! Wake up. Put your face in the sunlight. God's bright glory has risen for you." The vision of healing, of restoration, is accompanied by a vision of light shining in the darkness. And because the darkness, the suffering, has been so real, this new hope is no facile hope. It is the kind of hope that comes only after deep sorrow, a hope that still remembers the "cries of anguish" in the recent past.

John of Patmos, writing perhaps fifty to seventy years after Jesus's death, picks up all the themes discussed so far. He picks up the echoes of crisis, the battle between the powerful forces of this world and the forces of God, the judgment and victory of God's chosen servant, and the vision of a restored and healed city. Yet so often Revelation is misunderstood because, as Daniel before him, John wrote in images. At the heart of his vision, however, is the healing of the earth, the salvation of humanity, and the true worship of God. And indeed, John at the end paints a lovely and powerful picture.

It is an effort to paint a picture with words, an effort to put down on paper what one has seen in a vision. John writes in chapter 21:

> I saw Heaven and earth new-created. Gone the first Heaven, gone the first earth, gone the sea. I saw Holy Jerusalem, new-created, descending resplendent out of Heaven, as ready for God as a bride for her husband. I heard a voice thunder from the Throne: "Look! Look! God has moved into the neighborhood, making his home with men and women! They're his people; he's their God. He'll wipe every tear from their eyes. Death is gone for good—tears gone, crying gone, pain gone—all the first order of things gone."

It is a place, a place that U2 has also tried again and again to wrestle down into words, and to evoke in concerts throughout their career. It is, in a way, a glimpse into the shape of what Jesus longs for in his prayer: "your kingdom come, your will be done, on earth, as it is in heaven."

I Go There With You

Bono does not want to be confused with those who advocate leaving this world, longing for the end of time and heaven beyond. Apocalypse is not, for U2, about leaving this world behind for some other reality, but about getting a glimpse of the world as God desires it to be, a vision that guides and empowers us in our faithful struggle in the midst of the world. Speaking to a friend, Bono noted that:

> Zealots often have no love for the world. They're just getting through it to the next one. It's a favorite topic. It's the old cliché: "Eat s**t now, pie in the sky when you die." But I take Christ at his word: "On Earth as it is in Heaven."

And the roots of this compelling claim on Christ's words came out of the experience of trying to live those words.

Early in the 1980s, Bono, the Edge, and Larry Mullen Jr. (as I mention in the previous chapter, Adam was not a believer in their early years) joined an intentional Christian community called Shalom Fellowship. It was an intense experience Bono now describes as "a very well-thought out and finally flawed attempt to wrestle the world to the ground and try to deal with some of its ails and its evils." They lived at the time in a very ascetic way, living communally, with no possessions. But the leader eventually let the trio know that he felt the rock and roll life was incompatible with their faith. They considered breaking up the band, but after weeks of pondering the question, they instead came to the decision to leave Shalom. The ecstatic experience of charismatic worship marked them, however, and their songs sometimes evoke what communion with God through worship and prayer can be.

This kind of charismatic song led off their second record, recorded at the time of their spiritual crisis with Shalom. "Gloria" captures their confusion and struggle with the paradoxes of ascetic Christian community and the charging energy and life of a rock and roll band. The song idea came about when Bono was listening to some of manager Paul McGuiness's Gregorian chant records. The chorus, written and sung in Latin, offers transcendence, a reaching beyond this reality to another place where all the confusion and turmoil of this world is resolved in praise.

Musically, however, "Gloria" is no calm chant. It begins with descending drumbeats on the kit, and a rising single note on Edge's guitar. But mere seconds into the song, Bono shouts, "Two, three, four" and the band kicks into an upbeat tempo with a fat bass and very sharp guitar riff. The lyrics evoke confusion and searching: "I try to sing this song / I,

I try to stand up / But I can't find my feet. / I, I try to speak up / But only in you I'm complete." After almost stuttering, struggling to find the words (literally perhaps, given Bono's habit of improvising lyrics at the mike early on in their career), the last line surges forward into the chorus where some relief comes: "Gloria / In te domine / Gloria / Exultate / Gloria / Gloria / Oh, Lord, loosen my lips." The song opens a tradition that continues today where U2 substitutes "you" for "God" thereby making their love songs to God available as love songs generally. The song, while a perennial favorite in concert for its hard-charging music and soaring chorus, still betrays a sense of vulnerability, of incompleteness and longing, and the intimate grace of being drawn into an embrace of love. No matter the personal struggle of the one hearing this song, it is a ringing affirmation of God's calling us into the wholeness and healing that is God's deepest desire for the world. Gloria; what other response makes sense?

Two albums later, with the band more secure in their calling to be a band, and with a growing global audience, another lead-off song offered another vision of that other place. This song, too, has become a perennial concert favorite, and it has proven remarkably flexible and able to serve powerfully in a number of concrete circumstances. Bono wrote out of his experience as a child growing up in a very divided country. Writing in the band's official fan magazine when *The Joshua Tree* came out in 1987, Bono said:

"Where the Streets Have No Name," that's more like the U2 of old than any of the other songs on the LP. Because it's a sketch—I was just trying to sketch a location, maybe a spiritual location, maybe a romantic location, I was trying to sketch a feeling. I often feel very claustrophobic in a city, a feeling of wanting to break out of that city, a feeling of wanting to go somewhere where the values of the city and the values of our

society don't hold you down. An interesting story that somebody told me once, is that in Belfast, by what street somebody
lives on you can tell not only their religion, but tell how much
money they're making—literally by which side of the road they
live on . . . that said something to me, and so I started writing
about a place where the streets have no name . . ."

While the song has prophetic roots, obliquely critiquing the
values of our society, the inequality between rich and poor, it
does not primarily evoke those realities but transcends them by
evoking a vision of a place, another place, where those values
do not hold power. This was visually evoked through the song's
original video, shot on top of a storefront in the famously tough
neighborhood of South Central Los Angeles.

The song begins slowly with a single organ chord rising
in volume, and then slow shifting notes downward, joined
by the Edge's bouncing, jangling guitar line also rising in
volume, until a driving bass and drum pull the song into a
relentless run. The music almost says "I want to run" before
Bono comes in singing that first phrase of the song. "I wanna
run, I want to hide / I wanna tear down the walls / That hold
me inside. / I wanna reach out / And touch the flame / Where
the streets have no name." The feeling of claustrophobia, of
being trapped or held down by something, vibrates in this
first verse, and the desire to reach out, to touch the flame,
evokes the band's abiding spiritual connection to the spirit,
often imagined as a flame.

As if evoking the image of awaking to the bright sunlight of
God's glory from Isaiah 60:1 directly, Bono enters the second
verse singing: "I wanna feel sunlight on my face. / I see the dust-
cloud / Disappear without a trace. / I wanna take shelter / From
the poison rain / Where the streets have no name." The lyric
uses metaphor to evoke the difficulties of the world "the dust-
cloud" and the "poison rain." The lyric claims that we humans

99

seem never to make progress in learning to love; we are forever "building and burning down love." But the vision comes from a longing for more than struggle: "The cities a flood, our love turns to rust / We're beaten and blown by the wind, trampled in dust." The longing, finally, is for "a place where there's no sorrow or pain / Where the streets have no name."

This last line echoes both Isaiah and Revelation. It is a place beyond the transformation of the Son of Man, the one whose suffering transforms power and makes space for God's redemption to claim the victory. And in some concerts on tours during the 1990s, Bono would end the song with the lines, "Then will there be no time or sorrow / Then there will be no time, no shame." Very often this song provides a cathartic moment in the concerts, a place where their vision of concerts providing healing might be realized.

Such cathartic healing was certainly at the heart of the third leg of their Elevation tour in 2001 when their U.S. concerts took up the crisis and grief of the attacks on September 11. This reached its height in U2's amazing halftime show at the Super Bowl in January 2002. They agreed to do the show, despite the requirement that their roadies set up the heart-shaped stage in just six minutes. After a rousing opening with the hit single "Beautiful Day" from 2000's album *All That You Can't Leave Behind*, a huge screen behind the band began scrolling the thousands of names of those who died on September 11, accompanied by the haunting lullaby "MLK" that closed 1984's *Unforgettable Fire*. It is a brief song, meant in its own way to highlight that the ideals for which brave people die go on, even as we wish for sweet peace for those who, like Martin Luther King Jr., and like those who died that terrible day in September, are now gone: "Sleep, sleep tonight / And may your dreams be realized / If the thunder cloud passes rain / So let it rain, let it rain / Rain down on he."

As the strains of the last word faded, however, Edge's guitar chord rose out of the darkened stage. Bono could be heard quietly offering a prayer, drawing on Psalm 51, "Oh Lord, open my lips / So I might show forth thy praise / Oh Lord, open my lips / So I might show forth thy praise." And with a shout, "America," the song "Where The Streets Have No Name" flew into full speed. Images of dust and burning took on quite a different sense here, bringing to mind scenes from lower Manhattan on that tragic morning just four months prior. And as the song closed, with the last names rising off the top of the screen and the screen falling down below the rear of the stage, Bono made a heart out of his hands up against his chest and opened his coat to display the American flag. Absolute pandemonium filled the stadium and the band joined the applause, knowing they'd just been a part of something bigger than themselves.

The best example of the song's apocalyptic power, despite the high mark the Super Bowl performance represented for the band, is its role on their Vertigo tour in 2005–2006. Here, the song returns to its roots, but in a way that, for Bono at least, finally makes full sense of the song. In an interview while on tour in Chicago, he described their emphasis on helping end extreme poverty, especially in Africa, through promoting the idea of equality of all, not just those living in the West. In order to end extreme poverty, Bono helped create what is called the One campaign aiming at asking the wealthy nations of the world to raise their contributions to development aid to one percent of their GNP. Bono continued:

> So we took this notion, the journey of equality, and we start talking about it. This is our generation's challenge. So we thought about using flags as a backdrop during "Where the Streets Have No Name." I remember singing it the first night, it's not a very good lyric, though really great ideas are suggested

in the lyric, the idea that you could go on a journey to that other place. . . . Do you want to go to that other place? It puts the hair up on the back of my neck. Because we want to go to that other place. That lyric was written in a dusty field in northern Ethiopia. And I can finally make sense of it.

U2 has always been striving for that other place. On this tour, with this song, they may have found the most powerful leverage for their striving yet. To give you the feel for it, it might be best to just describe my experience of the concert, beginning with the song "Running To Stand Still," dedicated on this leg of the tour to the "proud men and women of the United States Army." The following, then, is from my review of the concert, written after their first gig in Boston in May of 2005.

"Running To Stand Still" began with Bono on harmonica and Edge on piano; it set a really different tone. People sang really well and loudly on the "la la la de day, la la la la de day, la la la de day" section of the song, and the rest of it, too, for that matter. What really caught me off guard, however, is the ending. The song is about heroin addicts in Dublin during a hard time, and how for some drugs seemed like the only way out of misery. So at the end of the song, after feeling the needle chill and the drug entering to do its work, Bono has gone into a chorus of Hallelujahs that make sense in terms of the relief of the addict's high. But here, as Bono moves into the Halle, halle, hallelujah, the UN Declaration of Human Rights begins scrolling on the huge main video screen and the crowd begins to cheer, and as they get to number three, a woman who seems to be East Asian reads the declarations, including numbers 3, 4, 5, and 6, with the last focusing on equality.

And from there, the band kicks into "Pride (In The Name of Love)." In the midst of it, Bono gets the crowd singing with him on the woo woo, oo oo's and keeps them going while he makes interjections like an African-American pastor that Dr. King's dream wasn't just about the American dream, and it is not just a European dream, or an Asian dream, but it is a dream about equality for the whole world, and the journey of equality moves on, with everyone being equal in the eyes of God, and especially Africans.

The song never ends; it just morphs into the beginning of "Where the Streets Have No Name" with its plucky, meditative guitar notes and Bono intoning connections between the bridge at Selma, important during the civil rights movement, and the mouth of the Nile, evocative of Africa's antiquity. He tells us that the journey of equality moves in an expansive direction, growing into a vision of equality for all. Then, instead of the typical beginning with a primal scream whaaaaaaaooooooooooh at the start of the song, here Bono calls upon South African–style shout, sort of like my old anti-apartheid tapes from *The Joshua Tree* era, and it went something like, ahhhh yeaaaa oooooh. And while this is going on musically, the light screens descend—two with large outlines of the continent of Africa and three scrolling with the flags of Africa. When the band kicked into full gear on this song, I felt the emotional rise of the movement of the concert overwhelm me, and I felt like I was going to fly. This, to make the worship analogy, is like the climax of Communion at the Easter Vigil, when so much else has built up through layers of conviction, confession, prayer and song, finally catching a vision of this heavenly banquet, this sacramental meal, where all are equal and all receive grace and mercy from God's loving hand. Call me a sucker or call me a true believer, but even though I knew this was coming, I was not prepared for the overwhelming emotional release of this song (which I love, to be sure, but in this context it connected it to such an enormous and awful situation as extreme poverty in Africa with a vision of healing and hope that just totally lifted my sights to what is possible).

Such moments are why Bono again and again describes music as a sacrament. It combines, as classical theology tells us, a material thing with the mighty promise of God. That experience, felt in the midst of a rock and roll concert, is indeed an apocalyptic vision; it is a vision of a "place, high on a desert plain." It is a place that, through our discipleship, we participate in bringing to earth, as it is in heaven.

U2 Songs Drawing on the Apocalyptic Voice

"Fire," "With a Shout," "October" (*October*); "Sunday Bloody Sunday" (*War*); "MLK" (*The Unforgettable Fire*); "Where the Streets Have No Name," "One Tree Hill," (*The Joshua Tree*); "Playboy Mansion" (*Pop*); "Love and Peace or Else" (*How to Dismantle an Atomic Bomb*)

Others?

STEP TWO . . .

7

SINGING THE CROSS

I'd be in big trouble if Karma was going to finally be my judge. I'd be in deep s**t. It doesn't excuse my mistakes, but I'm holding out for Grace. I'm holding out that Jesus took my sins onto the Cross, because I know who I am, and I hope I don't have to depend on my own religiosity. I love the idea of the Sacrificial Lamb. I love the idea that God says, "Look, you cretins, there are certain results to the way we are, to selfishness, and there's mortality as part of your very sinful nature, and, let's face it, you're not living a very good life, are you? There are consequences to actions." The point of the death of Christ is that Christ took on the sins of the world, so that what we put out did not come back to us, and that our sinful nature does not reap the obvious death. That's the point. It should keep us humbled. It's not our own good works that get us through the gates of heaven.

Bono

The Goal Is Soul

The heart of what makes U2 a great rock and roll band is their ability to connect to what is deepest in us. Bono has this written in shorthand on one of his guitars: "The goal is soul." During the Elevation tour, Bono would typically end the song "Beautiful Day" with a chant back and forth with the audience, singing "The goal is soul / soul / The goal is soul / soul." In one sense, such a phrase could be just schlock and no more. But if soul means something about spiritual depth, about mining the deepest and truest nature of people, then we've got something to work with. My proposal in this book is that a way to "sum up" the band's way of seeing the world and those things most important in life is through talking about a tradition of thinking about the Christian life called "the theology of the cross."

The theology of the cross is not just a perspective about Jesus, or about his death on the cross, although it is that. Rather, it is all about how you see the world, and therefore how you live in it. It is a perspective that shapes a way of life. Like most perspectives that shape our way of life, it is not just an idea. Rather, like Bono's reference to karma and grace above, it is a worldview, a way of framing and interpreting events and people in general. As I unfold this perspective, I'll first make some general comments about its shape, and then I'll say a few general things about how it relates to U2.

Sixteenth-century Reformation theologian Martin Luther, writing a defense of his so-called radical ideas about grace, challenged the standard perspectives of his day with this powerful statement that forms the heart of our exploration of this theological tradition: "A theologian of glory calls evil good and good evil. A theologian of the cross calls the thing what it actually is." In order to spell this out in as clear a manner as possible, let me start with a summary version of the two sides, and then spell each out in a bit more detail before I shift to see how U2 embodies this emphasis. The summary version of the theology of glory says our relationship to God depends on us; it is an "if, then" proposition. This is what Bono calls karma, and you might summarize it as "if you do good, God gives good to you." The summary version of the theology of the cross says our relationship to God depends on God; it is a "because, therefore" proposition. This is what Bono calls grace, and you might summarize it as "because Christ died for us, therefore God shows us unconditional love, forgiveness, and mercy." The theology of glory is in some sense predictable and amounts to an unremarkable extension of standard human expectation onto our image of God. The theology of the cross, however, is surprising and scandalous by human standards—only a merciful and loving God would have thought it up for us.

Theology of Glory

The theology of glory amounts to religious triumphalism, in the sense of religion as something we humans do. With roots in medieval scholastic theology, this perspective seeks to present a vision of God's glory modeled on an utterly human and highly optimistic accounting of human potential. First, it seeks to present the glory of God in terms that fulfill what are in fact fallen human standards for divine success: a God we can see, whose promises are certain and whose power is victorious. Second, such a theology of glory presents humanity in its most favorable light, suggesting that humans are able to see divine things through human intellect. Third, this overly optimistic view of human intelligence leads to an overly positive evaluation of human moral capacity, in that we are able to capture God's favor by our actions. In the end, we're left with a God who can be manipulated by a human project of self-mastery. And if that is the case, as St. Paul recognized long ago, we then have no need of the cross or the risen Christ. "If all we get out of Christ is a little inspiration for a few short years, we're a pretty sorry lot" (1 Corinthians 15).

While for the medieval church this approach translated into the practice of selling forgiveness (the practice that started Martin Luther's protest), today it shows up in understandings of the church as a prosperity pill, as "bless me" clubs (think, for example, of the best-selling book *The Prayer of Jabez*). The idea is that by faith and fitness, prayer and positive thinking, I will prosper and achieve my own little heaven on earth. In such a faith perspective, there are no room for ambiguities and doubts. God shows up in power for those whose lives exhibit a powerful faith. Successful thoughts lead to successful lives, and so things like sin and the cross, perceived as "downers," are left to the side. Such a perspective is all Easter and no Good Friday; it is all heaven and no earth; it is all faith and no doubt.

Theology of the Cross

As the great German theologian Jürgen Moltmann has said, "there is a good deal of support in the tradition for the theology of the cross, but it was never much loved." That U2 speaks from this "never much loved" tradition partly explains U2's rejection by certain groups of Christians. However, such a spiritual voice is exactly what makes U2 such a crucial voice for many God-seekers who are on the margins of the official religion — religion that, it ought to be said, is often more interested in capturing divine authority to put at the service of its own quite worldly power. Yet the theology of the cross *is* a central if neglected "key" in the "music" of the church over time. Found in St. Paul as well as (for example) in the life of St. Francis, in the early work of Martin Luther, and in such twentieth-century voices as Flannery O'Connor and Martin Luther King Jr. (among others), this perspective tends to fit well with those who are not satisfied with platitudes and false promises.

The theology of the cross is preferable not because it is easy but because it is true. Embracing the truth is not always easy. Theologian Gerhard Forde writes that the theology of the cross is "an offensive theology [because] it attacks what we usually consider the best in our religion." For example, Martin Luther observed, God is to be found precisely where theologians of glory are horrified to find the Almighty: as a child in a crib, as a criminal on a cross, as a corpse in a crypt. Sometimes it is tempting to want God to come in power. As U2 puts it in their 1997 song, "If God Will Send His Angels," we've got lots of troubles in this life, and "Hey, if God will send his angels / I sure could use them here right now." The truth is, however, that God does not show up in that way.

As theologian Robert Kolb puts it, "God reveals himself by hiding himself right in the middle of human existence." The truth is that no one has seen God, but Jesus of Nazareth, God in the flesh, has made God known to us—a God with holes in his hands, feet, and side. God, who has come near to us, is in the midst of our twisted and ruined existence. This God on the cross reveals the fullness of God's love as well as the inadequacy of all human efforts to "patch up life to please God."

Canadian theologian Douglas John Hall has spent a career mining the fruits of this theological tradition for a contemporary North American context. According to Hall, the theology of the cross "can't shut its eyes to all the things that are wrong with the world—and with ourselves, our human

111

selves, our Christian selves." Thus, such a perspective calls us to face the full truth of life, including the suffering. Only in acknowledging the presence of death and doubt does faith make any sense. There, we face the truth of life, of failure, of abandonment, of longing, all experienced by Jesus on the cross. Because the risen Christ bears the marks of the cross, the marks of facing suffering and death, our Christian life following the way of the cross is a path that "lightens the darkness" rather than repressing it.

While it centers on the cross, the theology of the cross is not just about Jesus's crucifixion, but rather a whole spirit and method of doing theology. An effective way to unpack this vision is through looking at St. Paul's conclusion in 1 Corinthians 13, where he wrote, "faith, hope, and love abide, and the greatest of these is love" (NRSV). Too often this passage is taken to be a sort of saccharine ode to romantic love and is thus read at many weddings. This would be the perspective of the theology of glory, interpreting this threesome as something already attained and on display in the happy couple.

But the passage looks quite different if we unpack it according to the theology of the cross—a tradition of reflection that St. Paul helped create in that very letter to the church in Corinth when in chapter one he said "For Jews demand signs and Greeks look for wonders, but we proclaim Christ crucified" (NRSV). It might seem disingenuous to say that U2, whose concerts have set the dramatic standard in rock and roll, are not about signs and wonders. Yet the fact is that this is not their core aim, as they sing in the song "Crumbs from Your Table," (*almost* quoting St. Paul) "you speak of signs and wonders / I need something other." *Mere* signs and wonders are not what U2 seeks here, despite the glamour of their rock cover. They are not seeking to be representatives of the theology of glory, despite what so many critics put on them. Rather than "signs and wonders," they "need something other." Could this "something other" be Christ crucified and the way of costly discipleship he asks us to follow?

"Brian? 'E's Not the Messiah! 'E's Just a Very Naughty Boy!"

It would be easy for Bono and U2 to accept the praise heaped onto them, even if some of it is praise couched in playful irony, as in the *Time* magazine cover article description of Bono as "the most secular of saints." Yet, despite the pretensions that come with being the biggest rock band in the world and having a social conscience to match, the band still refuses to take all the credit. They continue to point beyond themselves to some greater thing they have not—and cannot—achieve by themselves. In a tongue-in-cheek section of his book-length interview with music journalist Michka Assayas, Bono lampoons the temptation to glory for a rock and roll singer who crusades for the poor:

> So I actually have figured out that my best insurance from accusation of messianic behavior is to follow Monty Python to *The Life of Brian*. [Assayas: Which means?] When Brian walks out on the terrace and the people are calling his name, his mother walks out and goes: [shrill voice of an old common English woman] "Brian? 'E's not the Messiah! 'E's just a very naughty boy!"

In a very technical sense, this is exactly what Jürgen Moltmann is getting at when he writes:

> If [humanity] sees and believes God in the suffering and dying Christ, [humanity] is set free from the concern for self-

113

deification which guides [it] towards knowledge. Thus the knowledge of God in the Crucified Christ takes seriously the situation of [humanity] in the pursuit of [its] own interests, [humanity] who in reality is inhuman, because [it] is under the compulsion of self-justification, dominating self-assertion and illusionary self-deification.

Rather than take up illusions of grandeur regarding their accomplishments, U2 follows the way of the cross, calling for all who have ears to hear "to join the battle just begun" ("Sunday Bloody Sunday").

While they know the deepest truth of our lives is the reality of "faith, hope, and love," they still cry out (in the song "If God Will Send His Angels"): "So where is the hope and / Where is the faith and the love?" Lest anyone be quick to jump in and assert that things are not so bad, and love is all around if you look, U2 goes on to add a humorous poke at the shallowness of the culture of the West: "What's that you say to me / Does love light up your Christmas tree? / The next minute you're blowing a fuse / and the cartoon network turns into the news." Love, it turns out, is not power. Our faith is misplaced in our attraction to the glitter lighting up our Christmas trees and shopping malls. If we are to find hope in this world, that hope will not be grounded in something we can buy and possess. Neither will our faith be found in what we see on television.

Although it may mean times of spiritual wandering, seeking faith, hope, and love with U2 means going through the shopping malls and the television to find it. The next four chapters embody U2's sense that in seeking a way in the world that lifts up faith, hope, and love, one cannot simply run away from the world. In one of the most hilarious moments of their career, U2 made this point by announcing their 1997 PopMart tour at a New York City Kmart. Complete with a sign overhead that said, "Pop Group" and a nearby flashing blue light, they commented on the way their use of kitsch and popular culture icons simply gave a cover for their deeper convictions:

> In all honesty, we're still the bleeding hearts club, our music is painfully, insufferably earnest. We've just got really smart at disguising it, throwing people off that trail.

Asked what they thought of holding a press conference to announce a tour on Ash Wednesday at a Kmart, Bono responded, "Ash Wednesday and Kmart—that about wraps us up!" Ash Wednesday and Kmart, faith and the world; it is the theology of the cross that embodies the pattern of a God who became flesh and dwelt among us. Faith, hope, and love too, then, follow the path toward living in and for the sake of God's world.

8

FAITH (NOT SIGHT)

Belief and confusion are not mutually exclusive. I think belief gives you a direction in the confusion. But you don't see the full picture. That's the point. That's what faith is. . . . But you can't just rely on it. I'm sure you question your atheism, just as I question faith. You have to pummel it to make sure that it can withstand it, to make sure you can trust it.

Bono

What Is Faith?

That day in June, when I stood before the congregation, I couldn't get the words out. When I stood up, I fully intended to boldly say, "In our life together, I will be faithful and honest . . . from this day until my last." At the rehearsal, we'd left out practicing the vows, wanting to say them only once. Now, in the midst of the ceremony itself, Sonja, my lovely bride, held my hands and encouraged me. Somehow my body knew what an incredible promise I was making—that at age 24 I would pledge my life to this woman, only 22 herself. I did manage to say the lines, even if between tears and a croaky voice. But it was only as years went by that I fully understood why our pastor had titled her sermon "Audacious Promises." How could I know what the years would bring? How could I know the threats and challenges to such a commitment of faithfulness?

Yet, in fact, such promises made without knowing for sure the outcome in all its detail defines faith in the Christian tradition. Faith is not knowing but trusting nonetheless. In one of the classic formulations in scripture, Hebrews 11 states: "The fundamental fact of existence is that this trust in God, this faith, is the firm foundation under everything that makes life worth living. Its our handle on what we can't see." Faith, it turns out, is intertwined with the topic of the next chapter, hope. It is so because faith is trust, and the ability to trust is based on our hope of another's trustworthiness. We hope that those places we have judged trustworthy in fact turn out to be so, but we do not know for sure, not at the moment of our action in faith.

Faith, then, is by definition not certainty. Faith has at its heart longing and hope—longing for fulfillment and hope for what is promised. Yet faith lives on this side of fulfillment and does not yet have full possession of what is promised. In great biblical stories of faith, whether of Abraham and Sarah, Moses, or some other, the key components are God's offer of a promise and their trust, their faith, even though they do not now see how it will all turn out. So because of this reality—promise without fulfillment—faith is always accompanied by the presence of doubt.

It is much easier to understand the presence of doubt in the life of faith if the "who God is" question gets settled up front. For Christians, knowledge of God comes through Jesus, who lived in first-century Palestine, who was crucified for his actions and words, who died and after three days appeared alive to his disciples and friends. Without this beginning, the question of God might begin with some attributes derived from philosophy or natural observation. We might imagine that if we are limited in our power, God must be all-powerful. We could think that if we are limited in our intelligence, God who created all things surely knows all things. However, Christians don't come to know God through speculation, but in response to Jesus's declaration, "Repent, for the Kingdom of God is at hand!" and his invitation: "Follow me."

Christians, then, both know and don't know their God. God is a surprising God who, in spite of our human ideas of how a proper God should act, comes into the world as a helpless baby. The story of Jesus's birth—the divine child, the savior of the world, born in straw and surrounded by animals—is equally as unbelievable as his rejection and crucifixion thirty-three years later. Yet despite such surprises, there is a consistency to the Bible's portrayal of God's actions. God consistently acts on behalf of those who are in need—first of all in rescuing a group of slaves from Egypt and then afterwards teaching them to always remember and care for those among them who were vulnerable: the poor, the outcast, the widow.

God is portrayed as one who bears this rag-tag people, carrying them as a mother carries her child, and bearing with them as they struggle (and often fail!) to follow God's vision for living. And because Christians believe that Jesus was one with God, the "Son of God" in traditional language, God also bears Jesus's suffering and death. This means that Christians have faith in a God who knows our human experiences and sympathizes with the suffering of life. As German pastor and theologian Dietrich Bonhoeffer wrote while in one of Adolf Hitler's prisons, "Only the suffering God can help." Another German theologian, Jürgen Moltmann, struggling with these same questions, wrote:

> To recognize God in the crucified Christ means to grasp the Trinitarian history of God and to understand oneself and this whole world with Auschwitz and Viet Nam, with race-hatred and hunger, as existing in the history of God. God is not dead, death is in God. God suffers by us. God suffers with us. Suffering is in God.

The theology of the cross does not condone suffering, yet because God is with us, especially in suffering, we can be sustained in our struggle for a world in which suffering is no more. For that, most of all, is God's work—liberating, saving, healing, bearing, and dreaming of all creation made whole again.

Still Lookin'

As I noted in the introduction, I view U2 as an icon, that is, I see the band as pointing fans one step closer to the light that is the view of the soul. I do this because I think such a perspective makes a wider, fuller sense of the meaning of the band's words and lives. But that means that their songs and live performances need to echo this act of pointing to the soul of life, the deeper dimension where, in the midst of very ordinary things, the Spirit meets us and moves us and heals us. While we may have an image of God appearing in some predictably dramatic holy moment, the truth is that the God revealed in Jesus Christ actually chooses quite surprising ways and means.

For example, one night, just back in Dublin from years on the road with the ZooTV tour, Bono really got the Christmas story. Despite being critical of religion and the church over the years, Bono has still been a regular churchgoer, albeit in some unusual circumstances and at some unusual churches. Well, that Christmas Eve Bono went to St. Patrick's Cathedral with some of his Church of Ireland friends. As he recalls it, he had a bad seat, behind a huge pillar. Picking up the story, he remembers having some trouble staying awake:

> Being up for a few days, traveling, because it was a bit boring, the service, and I just started nodding off, I couldn't see a thing. Then I started to try and keep myself awake studying what was on the page. It dawned on me for the first time, really. It had dawned on me before, but it really sank in: the Christmas story. The idea that God, if there is a force of Love and Logic in the universe, that it would seek to explain itself is amazing enough. That it would seek to explain itself and describe itself by becoming a child born in straw poverty, in s**t and straw . . . a child . . . I just thought: "Wow!" Just the poetry . . . Unknowable love, Unknowable power, describes itself as the most vulnerable. There it was. I was sitting there, and its not that it hadn't struck me before, but tears came down my face, and I saw the genius of this.

While many look for God in glitter, success, and heavenly thoughts, the God of Jesus Christ is found in situations of poverty, vulnerability, pain, and suffering. And while such faith always seems fragile in relation to the powers of this world, it is a faith that has echoed throughout the songs of U2's catalog.

In one sense, this is at the heart of their first album, *Boy*. It is an album that tries to make transparent the vulnerability of innocence and the confusion of its passing. But it is also an album that goes directly into the space of confusion at its hardest, the place of suffering where it hurts the most, in search of faith to go on. Both Bono and Larry lost their mothers at a young age. Their first single from the album *Boy*, "I Will Follow," draws on this well of creative vulnerability. And despite its obvious longing, it also is an affirmation of faith. Writing about his mother's death, Bono sings: "A boy tries hard to be a man / His mother takes him by the hand / If he stops to think, he starts to cry / Oh why?" Yet despite the obvious trauma the death of his mother caused, there is a tenacity of faith that he is not finally alone in his sorrow. Echoing the old gospel tune "Amazing Grace," the song declares with confidence, "I was lost, I am found / If you walk away, walk away / If you walk away, walk away / I will follow."

Issues of faith and loss came to the fore again in a profound way a few years ago as Bono's father, Bob, was dying of cancer. It struck Bono as ironic that while his father had lost his faith, "he seemed to think this was the most important thing I had to offer. In fact, it was what he liked best about the band: our faith." Yet Bono's father, like so many of U2's fans, was unable to see how one could "pummel" faith, or even shout at God, as an act of faith. And that was just what they did. U2 set a course for the 1990s that amounted to the journey of Ecclesiastes, "dancing with their doubts and testing their temptations," without ever losing their way back home. Rather than irreligious, the band felt that their work in the 1990s was rooted in the same core values—including their faith—that had led them to that point, even if the vehicle for delivering the ideas had changed. While his own father didn't see it, Bono said that:

> On *Pop*, I thought it was a tough relationship with God that was described there: "Looking for to save my, save my soul / Looking in the places where no flowers grow / Looking

122

for to fill that God-shaped hole." That's a quite interesting lyric, because that's the real blues—that comes from Robert Johnson, it happens through the machine age, through this techno din, but there it is: the same yearning.

On an album named "Pop," a song that digs as deep as a Robert Johnson blues tune seems totally out of place. But as Bono remarked, the idea was to have music with a lightweight quality while adding a lyric that is not emotionally shallow. "We've had to get the brightly colored wrapping paper right, because what is underneath is not so sweet."

"Mofo," the song from Pop that describes the "God-shaped hole," is a prime example of a general principle with U2: people may just groove on the vibe of the music, but if they listen to the lyric, it might just hit home, pointing below or beyond the surface of material glitter that is rock and roll. This was especially so on the PopMart tour that kicked off in Las Vegas, the capital of glitter! In such searching lyrics, it seems Bono intended exactly to say, well, your experience may be only confusion amidst all the glitter of life, but if you find a moment to reflect, you will likely find a hole suffering has put in your life just as I have in mine. Indeed, he commented to Neil McCormick:

> Everyone's got one. Some are blacker and wider than others. It goes right back to the blues, it's what first makes you want to shout at God, when you've been abandoned or someone's been taken away from you. And I don't think you ever fill it, not completely. You can fill it up with time, by living a full life, but if you're silent enough, you can still hear the hissing.

From the perspective of the theology of the cross, one might say God as well had such a hole, a hole created by taking the suffering and sin of the world into God's own heart. Rather

123

than saving us by divine fiat, pulling us out of difficult situations, we find God meets us in our vulnerable places, joins with us in our confusion, and carries us in our suffering.

Attributing such high-minded thoughts to a song titled "Mofo" which, very clearly, the band meant as shorthand for the term "motherf**ker," may strain your generosity as a reader. Let me assure you that it is what it is, and I don't know all the reasons why they used it. But let me say something, for it exactly relates to the theme of the theology of the cross and its critique of theology of glory, and therefore why Jesus had to be born in "s**t and straw" rather than silk. The term is, as are so many other references on the album, part of popular culture. Thus, in one sense, its use is a throwaway gesture to trashy language, to a kind of shallowness and even crassness in culture. Bono seems to have wanted that, musically and lyrically.

Musically, they had originally created an almost Motown-style R&B style for the song. It was even finished, and people really liked it. But the song didn't fully match the way Bono had written a lyric that was "both precious and trashy." So working with their 1990s producers Flood and Howie B, they emptied out the song, added a double beat, and built from there, ending up with what Bono calls a "techno carnival." And the lyric captures the tensions between divergent styles within one band by portraying the tensions with word pictures such as this version of theology of the cross in miniature: "Looking for the baby Jesus under the trash."

It is a song that portrays the band's searching spirituality grounded in the conviction that God is somehow found by looking at the world rather than running from it. But they still believe that God will come, God will be present in the midst of life. Near the end of the song, they hint at this doubting faith when they sing, "Lookin' for a sound that's gonna drown out the world / Lookin' for the father of my two little girls. / Got the swing, got the sway, got my straw in lemonade. / Still lookin' for the face I had before the world was made. Mother, mother-suckin' rock an' roll." Still looking, and sure that *what* they are looking for is to be found: a promise of something pure, healed, whole—as things were in the time "before the world was made." "Mofo" is, one might say, a hymn of serious *and* playful faith that still searches and doubts.

It was not, however, their first hymn of doubt. This came a decade prior on *The Joshua Tree*. They had been listening to a lot of gospel music, but the album had coalesced around the arid symbol of the desert. The idea, however, was not that the desert is empty. Rather, they were after the notion that it is clarifying, that things are stark there, and that among other things it is spiritually trying. Early on in the process of working on the song eventually titled "I Still Haven't Found What I'm Looking For," U2 felt that they wanted to focus the song on spiritual doubt. As Bono said at the time of the album's release, "*The Joshua Tree* is a very uncertain record. 'I Still Haven't Found What I'm Looking For' is an anthem of doubt more than faith." And this song, more than anything up to that point, caused a certain group of Christians to write the band off as lost. Called "Squeakers" by the band, these Christians seemingly can't survive in close proximity to the world. They don't drink, swear, engage with unseemly people, and never admit doubt. Yet for U2, such black-and-white Christianity nearly led to their demise as a group, and to their abandonment of their God-blessing as a band. So this song, and its theme of seeking out God in the midst of a desert, not only has scriptural echoes of Moses and the people wandering in the wilderness, but also of Jesus on numerous occasions when he went into the wilderness seeking focus and God's voice through the clarity of the desert.

125

The song, while offending some of U2's "Squeaker" constituency, opened itself to a much broader demographic: those who, like me, feel compelled to look at the suffering in the world and find there plenty of reason to embrace a faith that doubts, a faith that still looks for more. The song begins with a rising volume of Edge's guitar picking in almost bell-like tones. But immediately, as well, the gospel sound comes across in the shaking tambourine. The lyric makes one feel the strength of striving after the one desired (here, again, U2 uses the ploy of speaking of God as "you" so that it becomes more inclusive in meaning and connection).

> I have climbed the highest mountains / I have run through the fields / Only to be with you / Only to be with you. / I have run, I have crawled / I have scaled these city walls / These city walls / Only to be with you.

Yet seeking and trusting the promise of what is to be found does not mean that they have found fulfillment in their seeking. All is not made whole. All is still not well in the world. And so, they sing "But I still haven't found / What I'm looking for."

Thus far in the song, the references are vague and could have been about a search for a lover (like many other U2 songs!). With the exception of *October*, where their faith was much more on display, U2 has not usually made explicit confessions of faith in their songs. Yet here, in their anthem of doubt, they offer perhaps the most explicit confession of faith in any single song they've done:

> I believe in the Kingdom Come / Then all the colors will bleed into one / Bleed into one. / But yes, I'm still running. / You broke the bonds / And you loosed the chains / Carried the cross of my shame / Of my shame, you know I believe it.

126

Here is the core of the Christian faith, and its orientation to faith in the coming of God's promised reign, a coming that is only possible through the suffering of the cross. It is as if they say, "Yes!" "But!" "But I still haven't found / What I'm looking for." I'll say more about the dynamic of knowing the *now* of salvation and yet hoping for its fulfillment in God's future in chapter eleven.

As the band was preparing to go on tour through the United States in support of *The Joshua Tree*, U2's record label received a tape of a gospel choir's cover version of "I Still Haven't Found What I'm Looking For." As the Edge said at the time, "it sounded like, totally different, but it sounded really exciting, new, so we traveled down to Harlem and visited this church in the middle of Harlem where this church was running through a rehearsal and we got this idea of doing a combination version." The gospel group, New Voices of Freedom, began covering this song in their concerts and sent a tape of it to U2. When U2 came through New York on tour, they went to visit the church and tried out singing the song together. Bono tells the story this way:

> We'd never done this before, you know, we arrived at the church in Harlem, we went through the rehearsal, and we thought, like, let's just go for it, let's see what happens, so the choir comes down to our show at Madison Square Gardens. And they come on stage and the first thing we realize is if Adam or Larry or myself play at full volume no one is going to hear them so we start playing, like literally, just tapping the strings and the drums. So that was fine and they started up and it was like brilliant, and so towards the end, we stopped playing altogether and they just took over and to see the choir and the audience all singing together—Ahh! We just stood on the side of the stage with our mouths open. Wow, what an experience!

127

The pieces of their faith combine: powerful and moving and truthful music, sung in a way that both admits the limits of life and yet in word and deed gives a vision of something more. An African-American gospel choir on stage with an Irish rock band, singing faith, singing doubt, singing as one. The vision offered in that moment gives hope. And it is hope that I turn to in the next chapter.

U2 Songs Embodying Themes of Faith and Doubt

"I Will Follow", "Twilight" (*Boy*); "Jerusalem" (*October*); "I Still Haven't Found What I'm Looking For" (*The Joshua Tree*); "Love, Rescue Me" (*Rattle and Hum*); "Mofo" (*Pop*); "Elevation" (*All That You Can't Leave Behind*)
Others?

9

Hope (Not Possession)

The most powerful idea that's entered the world in the last few thousand years—the idea of grace—is the reason I would like to be a Christian. Though, as I said to The Edge one day, I sometimes feel more like a fan, rather than actually in the band. I can't live up to it. But the reason I would like to is the idea of grace. It's really powerful.

Bono

What Is Hope?

When my wife Sonja was pregnant with our first child (we didn't then know it was a boy), I had a dream that he or she would be born with a severe handicap. I didn't have the dream just once, either. While this dream was very unsettling, I tried to tell myself it would be okay. I thought, well, my life has been so good and we have so much love and support to offer, why not us? We did not do any of the available prenatal testing, but Sonja was very sick for most of the pregnancy. (Morning sickness? How about 24/7 sickness!) Deep down I worried that this confirmed my dreams. When she finally did go into labor that March morning, we just focused on the task at hand, and by evening we held Isaiah in our arms—a healthy, normal, full-term baby boy.

While I don't think I'm any great model to hold up, this simple story does help illustrate the difference between a cultural sense of hope—better described as optimism—and hope in the Christian tradition. Friends to whom I told my dream thought I was being crazy, and they told me not to be so pessimistic. They thought I was not being hopeful because I was not imagining that things would turn out entirely well. In the United States, especially, and likely to some extent in Western countries influenced by American culture, hope is almost equated with the power of optimism, the "power of positive thinking" to quote the title of the popular book by pastor Norman Vincent Peale. Douglas John Hall, a Canadian theologian, has described the United States as a culture of "official optimism." At times, it felt like some acquaintances *required* me to be hopeful—read "optimistic"—about the outcome of the pregnancy.

At the heart of the theology of the cross lies another understanding of hope altogether. Hall describes it this way: "Hope, as it is conceived under the sign of the cross, isn't based on the capacity of humans (some of them) to think positively, cheerfully, and hopefully. It's based on faith in God's grace and providence." Indeed, at some deep level, I felt a calm. On the one hand, the dreams about a child with a severe handicap were worrisome, and I knew that it was indeed a real possibility. On the other, my hope—for this child as for the world—came from faith in a God who loves us deeply, who suffers in the midst of the world's brokenness in order to mend and redeem it. Hope comes from what God is doing, as a gift and out of love. Whatever I would do as a parent would be an extension of that gift of hope rather than my own optimism, and such a hope is enough to bear all things.

In his wonderful book *What's So Amazing About Grace?*, author Philip Yancey notes how surprised people are when they realize how often Jesus spent time with sinners and outcasts. Yancey writes:

> Having spent time around "sinners" and also around purported "saints," I have a hunch why Jesus spent so much time with the former group: I think he preferred their company. Because the sinners were honest about themselves and had no pretense, Jesus could deal with them. In contrast, the saints put on airs, judged him, and sought to catch him in a moral trap. In the end it was the saints, not the sinners, who arrested Jesus.

Who Jesus was, and what he taught, according to the theology of the cross, constitutes our most sure knowledge of God. True knowledge of God (and therefore hope) comes from knowing that in Christ God comes near to us in mercy and love. True knowledge of God, that is, comes from knowing grace.

It follows, therefore, that the theological category that most makes sense of Christian hope is not optimism; it is grace. The road to receiving grace requires honesty, and for many of us the road to honesty leads through humiliation. Not that our humiliation is the point—wholeness is, and abundant life with God! But for too many of us, dishonesty in relation to our inhumanity is preferable to painful honesty. And the seductive nature of the theology of glory comes in just here. In an effort to prove our worth, we puff ourselves up and seek to maintain our lives in that inflated form that we imagine is worthy of God, or some other standard we hold in highest esteem. Yet deep underneath, we fear we'll be found out, that we don't measure up. Such fear produces a cycle of defensiveness and judgment to assure oneself and others that indeed the puffed-up self is really what it seems. Such optimism is not only a false view of humanity, but more important, it gets the God of Jesus Christ wrong as well. As Bono advised fellow rocker Noel Gallagher of Oasis, "Go to God, tell him what all your flaws are and say, 'Can you work with me?'" God can stand our faults; it is we who can't stand to admit them.

It is key to state clearly that hope—and its reason for being, grace—are not concepts that tell us about humanity or the world; they first of all speak of God. The best understandings of grace come in Jesus's parables. Too often, parables are presented as one more means for us to shape ourselves up before God. As such, they supposedly teach us about the need to persevere, to be humble, to forgive, or to be grateful. Are the parables merely wise guides for living? They are not. Rather, as Philip Yancey puts it, Jesus gave the parables "to correct our notions about who God is and how God loves."

Perhaps the best-known parable of grace is a story of a father and his two sons found in the Gospel of Luke (I tell the story in chapter four above). Many people will know the story from a moralistic perspective as the story of the son who demands his inheritance and then spends it all on wine, women, and song. But Philip Yancey is right—the parable would be better titled, "The Prodigal God." The point of the parable is summed up in the words of the spiritual writer Henri Nouwen:

> God rejoices. Not because the problems of the world have been solved, not because all human pain and suffering have come to an end, nor because thousands of people have been converted and are now praising him for his goodness. No, God rejoices because *one* of his children who was lost has been found.

132

The offense of Jesus's attention to sinners is modeled on this portrayal of God's embarrassing willingness to run in a totally undignified manner to embrace the unworthy son who has returned.

Such an image of God is of little interest to those so sure they are righteous (like the older son in the parable) that they believe themselves to be near God. They would find it distasteful, to say the least, to have to seek mercy from such an ungodly God. But those who, like the prodigal son, know their own capacity to waste an inheritance, to live seeking their own pleasure alone, and to discard concern for others in the process, such mercy is nothing short of a miracle. St. Paul points to the heart of grace and the hope that flows from it: "God put his love on the line for us by offering his Son in sacrificial death while we were of no use whatever to him" (Romans 5:8). The age-old story of human life is a story of "ungrace," according to Yancey, and of God's wrath at such wasting of the gift of abundant life offered through the creation of each of our lives and of the whole world.

In his powerfully moving book *Free of Charge*, theologian Miroslav Volf writes about how he came to understand the necessity of seeing God as full of wrath at our actions in the world. He didn't think wrath was worthy of the God of love. "Shouldn't divine love be beyond wrath?" he thought. But the last vestiges of his resistance to this idea fell under the horror of the war in the former Yugoslavia, where he was born and raised. With hundreds of thousands killed and brutalized, and millions displaced, he writes that he could not imagine God not being angry. God's love *causes* God to be angry at humanity's inhumanity. God's anger, God's wrath, then, is the right response to the "ungrace" of human evil.

Many gods throughout history have been the sort that would demand justice and punishment, and who would exact vengeance against such human "inhumanity." Such an act would play right into the human theology of glory that expects our good will be repaid by blessing, and our bad will be repaid with punishment. Rather, the God we know in Jesus Christ forgives by becoming the one punished "for us." Christ, as God in human form, takes on himself the rejection, suffering, and death that human sin has caused. And the deepest mystery of faith, proclaimed by Jesus's disciple Peter, is this: "You pinned him to a cross and killed him. But God untied the death ropes and raised him up. Death was no match for him" (Acts 2). Though killed unjustly, God introduces divine justice into the midst of this present world. And we humans, caught as we are in webs of injustice, find freedom and hope through participation in Christ's death and rising. Jürgen Moltmann puts it this way: "In the crucified Jesus the 'end of history' is present in the midst of the relationships of history. Therefore in him can be found reconciliation in the midst of strife and hope for overcoming the strife." In dying on the cross, Jesus faces human inhumanity in a confrontation. The point, then, is to place in history a sign of God's future overcoming of all "ungrace" with grace, or as John's Gospel put it poetically, a light shining in the darkness that the darkness could not overcome. Without fully facing the darkness, God's gift of light would bring shallow hope. But without the grace of God in Christ facing the darkness "for us," we would have no hope at all.

It's Who You Know That Gets You Through

In one sense the theology of the cross is grim; and yet in another sense it is so full of an embrace of the world, of life, and of hope that it is quite surprising. The truth is that while much religion, Christianity included, has focused on getting people from earth to heaven, the theology of the cross is about the power of God's coming to earth. God, as it were, conspired to give us hope for the abundant life God intended in creation through coming in the most shocking way: as a babe in a manger, as a wandering preacher, as a dying convicted criminal. And all this, truly, was to reform us into the image of God so that we might take our proper place as co-conspirators of hope for the sake of the world.

In imagining their role in this work on behalf of the troubles of the world, whether in Northern Ireland, Sub-Saharan Africa, or in one's own heart, U2 understands themselves to be part of God's work shining light in the darkness. "An old but very wise man once said to me that you should never fight darkness with light, you should just try to make the light brighter," Bono said in an interview.

> You see things going on out there and you think, "Well, what the hell can I do about it?" For a lot of people there's not a lot you can do about it and all I believe is that everyone in their own way has a position they have to take and if that's as a mother with snotty nosed kids or a guy in a factory just doing the best he can or being a schoolteacher or a farmer, you just find your ground, your place and you just do the best you can to shine a light on the s**t that's out there. . . . I'm in a band and I just hope that when it's all over for U2 that in some way we've made the light a bit brighter. Maybe just tore off a corner of the darkness.

I'll have more to say about how U2 has indeed "made the light a bit brighter" in chapter twelve, but here I'll need to show how this understanding of hope plays in U2's songbook.

An interesting place to start is a song directly about light, but fitting for the 1990s mood of U2, the title refers to a black light: "Ultraviolet (Light My Way)." The song was never released as a single and didn't feature much beyond the ZooTV tour that followed *Achtung Baby*, where "Ultraviolet" was the tenth track, yet it is a classic U2 track both musically and lyrically. Beginning with soft synthesizers and a singing, almost breathing, sighing, crying sound, Bono comes in with a solo on the lines: "Sometimes I feel like I don't know / Sometimes I feel like checking out. / I want to get it wrong / Can't always be strong / And love, it won't be long." Boom, in comes the full band in a familiar U2 groove. Immediately the song has introduced the main themes of doubt and faith, love and longing. Struggling to be faithful, the song pleads for help from one whose obvious sadness over the state of things adds poignancy to the relationship.

> Oh, sugar, don't you cry. / Oh, child, wipe the tears from your eyes. / You know I need you to be strong / And the day it is dark, as the night is long. / Feel like trash, you make me feel clean. / I'm in the black, can't see or be seen.

The chorus turns toward pleading for help, "Baby, baby, baby, light my way. / Alright now, baby, baby, baby, light my way." Fans have found in this a song like so many others in U2's catalog: it could be sung to God, and it could be sung to a lover. One U2 fan traced the line, "Your love was a light bulb hanging over my bed" to the book of Job, where God serves as a lamp shone upon Job's head and a light for walking through darkness.

Such a longing for love to light a way through the darkness fits a more plaintive lover's mood, but at times anger at the world's darkness comes boiling up and the lyric demands more. In a blistering tribute to John Lennon's tune, "God," which U2 recorded on their *Rattle and Hum* album and movie, U2 gives no doubt as to their sympathy with Lennon. In the song, Lennon strips away everything his

136

fans might cling to, and especially the glories of the Beatles era. U2, however, turns Lennon's dismissal of commitment or belief in his song into their own claim of hope, active in love. Titled "God Part II," they borrow a lyric from singer Bruce Cockburn about kicking the darkness. The verse goes, "Don't believe in the sixties / The golden age of pop / You glorify the past / When the future dries up. / Heard a singer on the radio / Late last night / Says he's gonna kick the darkness / Till it bleeds daylight. / I, I believe in love." U2 and Bruce Cockburn shared a deep concern about United States policy in Central America that, for U2, came out most powerfully in "Bullet the Blue Sky." Here, though, this anger connects with a key way hope is articulated in U2's work as a band.

Such a view of hope is one side of the equation, for it is the way one looks at the world after one has found, or been found by, grace. This view *remembers suffering* even as it has been claimed by grace for a vision of the world healed of its suffering. While on Easter Sunday Jesus was raised by God to new life, he embraced the disciples with hands still marked by the nails of the cross. Bono recently commented on this view of people and the world, making the point that while it is hopeful, it is not naïve:

> Look: evil encroaches in tiny footsteps on every great idea. And evil can almost outrun most great ideas, but finally, in the end, there is light in the world. I accept God chooses to work with some pretty poor material. But I'm much more amazed by what people are capable of than I am by what they're not capable of, which is to say evil doesn't surprise me. . . . Just because I often find a way around the darkness doesn't mean that I don't know it's there. I just try to make the light brighter.

The other half of the equation is how the light came to be in the world at all. For that, we'll need to shift to different sorts of songs, songs that are no less real about the darkness of our lives but that focus on telling the truth about the source of our hope.

One of the most obvious bits of proof that the theology of the cross is not just stark but also hilarious, good-natured, and in love with the world in a playful way, can be found through a quick reading of the lyric for *Pop's* "Playboy Mansion." While the song was largely ignored by critics and never played live, the song is among the most theologically profound. The title might give you the impression that the song is shallow—all about money, sex, and male ego. It is, but that is only half of the meaning, and not the deeper layer. Derek Walmsley, an Anglican priest in Yorkshire, describes the song beautifully in the book *Get Up Off Your Knees*, a collection of sermons drawing on U2 lyrics. It is no less than a hymn to grace.

The song begins with a sort of wah-wah guitar and slow drum beat. The music has a swaying feel, and when he begins to sing, Bono's voice caries the mood forward with a vocal at once subdued yet persistent in its questioning. Questioning what? How does one get through the gates of the mansion. Which mansion? Well, that's exactly the question. The album as a whole plays with the shallowness of popular culture, from an opening song that is a paean to bubble-gum love ("Discothèque") to a searing erotic portrayal of desire ("If You Wear That Velvet Dress"). And "Playboy Mansion," after opening with a parade of the cultural icons of consumer society (Coke, Michael Jackson, plastic surgery, O. J. Simpson, the Big Mac, the perfume Obsession, talk shows as confession), Bono asks longingly but doubtfully, "What am I to do? / Have I got the gifts to get me through / the gates of that mansion?"

In celebrity society, success is measured in prestige, in money, and the cachet of the brand name.

How does one gain access to the mansion, to the place of our desire, where everything is pleasure? As the verses go on, Bono explores the religious options in pop culture, including lotto and gambling in our modern-day cathedrals—casinos. In this world, he sings, "chance is a kind of religion / where're you're damned for plain hard luck." However, as the middle of the song comes, we find a shift that begins to ask questions about which mansion is at issue. "Love, come on down," Bono sings. "Let my numbers come around." Is this longing for luck? Is it hope for fame and wealth?

No, he's waiting for a time when "the colors come flashing / And the lights go on. / Then will there be no time for sorrow / Then will there be no time for shame." Ah, now the vision of that other mansion comes into view. Jesus talked about "the many rooms in my Father's mansion." It is an image of heaven, an image from Revelation 21 common in U2 songs since "Sunday Bloody Sunday," portraying a time and place where sorrow and shame are no more. While so many try to buy their way into the mansions of this world, they fit right into the theology of glory. It is an approach that seeks to storm the gates of heaven only to find out that they are locked. No one, St. Paul argues, not one is worthy. All have fallen short. None of our efforts, and not even luck, will get us into *that* mansion.

So how does one gain access to *that* mansion, the place beyond sorrow and shame? It is in fact quite like the worldly mansions. The song ends by hinting at the answer: "We'll go driving in that pool / It's who you know that gets you through / The gates of the playboy mansion." Jesus, in John chapter 14, says how to get in: he says it is through knowing him. In God's gift of grace, known in Jesus Christ, we find ourselves given the access. It is through "that pool" of baptism that we die with Christ and are raised to newness of life. It is through the gift of grace that we now have friendship with God. We are not doomed to a karmic universe where what you give out comes back to you in equal measure. We don't get what we deserve; we get what God offers. As Bono put it in a recent interview, "It's not our own good works that get us through the gates of heaven." Right. Our hope is that grace will get us through.

In the week after my daughter Grace was born on Halloween, 2000, three friends gave us copies of *All That You Can't Leave Behind*. The last track, a tune titled "Grace," both imagines grace as an idea and as "a name for a girl." It turns out that "Amazing Grace" is Bono's favorite hymn. Hints of its lyrics blend into the band's early hit single, "I Will Follow." And they have played some of the song in concert a dozen times over the years, including in a series of emotional concerts in Europe just after the London bombings in the summer of 2005. The heartfelt and emotional placement in these concerts—"Amazing Grace" is sung at the end of "Running to Stand Still" as the Declaration of Human Rights scrolls up the video screens—makes good on the claim that "grace makes beauty out of ugly things."

The song "Grace" starts with a simple guitar and bass line, picking out the tune cleanly at a tempo that doesn't hurry and doesn't linger, either. Almost a washing sound comes in from a synthesizer (you can hear the influence of Brian Eno here). Then Bono enters with the lyric's strength all at once—not building to the more explicit religious language, as is so often the case in U2 songs. "Grace, she takes the blame / she covers the shame / removes the stain." Then the song, which in typical U2 form gives a female sense to divine personae, seems to actually have a person in mind. Grace is the name of a girl, walking on a street, and you can hear music as she walks. At the time when U2 was putting the album together, Bono was active in the Jubilee 2000 campaign and had been touring Africa with various politicians and aid groups. While in Kampala, the capital of Uganda, he met Grace Nawakunde who, while struggling with AIDS herself, led a drama and singing group in the poorer neighborhoods of the city. They teach people through story and song how to protect themselves from AIDS. Bono recalls his first impressions meeting Grace:

> I asked, "where do these women get their passion from?" I was told they're all HIV-positive themselves. I looked at them. They were singing with such great joy. I thought "how could this be?" Then I realized . . . these are the firemen running up the building. These are the heroes of the day. And they know, all of them, they're going to die because they can't afford the dollar a day that it would take to keep them alive.

Grace indeed makes music in the streets, music that makes "beauty out of ugly things." Uganda, in no small part because of Grace and groups like hers, has halved the AIDS infection rate over the last decade and become a model for other African nations.

Grace is not just a person in the song; it is also "an idea that changed the world." The song takes up a favorite theme of the band, placing grace over against the idea of karma. Karma, that age-old idea that we get what we deserve, would leave us all in a bad way. Grace, however, makes the case for a God of mercy who is the logic at the heart of the universe that, in the words of author Philip Yancey, makes for "atrocious mathematics." While according to the standards of the world God's ways seem unfair, the logic of grace is that we don't get what we deserve. This is the message Jesus preached as the key to the kingdom of heaven, and in one parable he compared it—as U2 does in this song—to "a pearl in perfect condition." Jesus said, "God's kingdom is like a jewel merchant on the hunt for excellent pearls. Finding one that is flawless, he immediately sells everything and buys it" (Matthew 13). Not that we can find it; it is given to us, and our only task is to "sell everything and buy it" which is to say, open our hands and receive.

The receiving changes us, however. As the song "Grace" ends, it hints at just how we are changed, recalling the prophecy of Isaiah. The song ends poetically, even hopefully, if I might return to the theme of this chapter without being at all saccharine about it. "What once was hurt / What once was friction / What left a mark / No longer stings / Because Grace makes beauty / Out of ugly things." Such a claim does not erase the ugly; rather it claims the promise that because of Christ, God sees differently, and where there is hurt, a mark, a stain, God covers and heals and makes whole. "If your sins are blood-red, they'll be snow-white; If they're red like crimson, they'll be like wool," sings the poet-prophet Isaiah in chapter 1. Therefore, as one made white as snow, as one healed, live so healed. "Say no to wrong, work for justice, help the down and out, stand up for the homeless, go to bat for the defenseless," sings Isaiah. Grace offers hope, real hope, because grace enlists us in God's conspiracy of hope. As Bono once said, "I love the phrase, 'the conspiracy of hope', and I would like U2 to be remembered as being a part of something like that."

U2 Songs Embodying Themes of Hope

"Tomorrow" (*October*); "New Year's Day" (*War*); "God Part II" (*Rattle and Hum*); "Ultraviolet (Light My Way)" (*Achtung Baby*); "Miss Sarajevo" (*Passengers: Original Soundtracks 1*) "Playboy Mansion" (*Pop*); "When I Look at the World" (*All That You Can't Leave Behind*)
Others?

10

LOVE (NOT POWER)

My understanding of the Scriptures has been made simple by the person of Christ. Christ teaches that God is love. What does that mean? What it means for me: a study of the life of Christ. Love here describes itself as a child born in straw poverty, the most vulnerable situation of all, without honor. I don't let my religious world get too complicated. I just kind of go: Well, I think I know what God is. God is love, and as much as I respond *[sighs]* in allowing myself to be transformed by that love and acting in that love, that's my religion. Where things get complicated for me, is when I try to live in this love. Now, that's not so easy.

Bono

What Is Love?

I've noticed something happening more often recently as I drive around town. I'll be at an intersection, waiting at a stoplight. Sometimes I'm on my bike, sometimes in the car, but it doesn't seem to matter. I'll be waiting at the stoplight and I'll look across to see the car opposite me with its left blinker on. The light will change to green, and the car will leap out to make the turn in front of me. I've had some close calls in these situations because I tend to feel the impulse to surge forward myself. I have the occasional righteous fantasy that my old Toyota Corolla will be smashed by some overeager driver and I'll get to buy myself a shiny new car on their dime.

I imagine that my fantasy is righteous because I believe in some childish way that it is "my turn," and by going first, these overeager drivers step on my rights. I imagine them to be either people with overly large egos, rushing to meet their next obligation, or people with crushed egos, taking advantage of this relatively simple means to win at some game in life. Either way, I imagine, they are to be pitied as self-centered and therefore by definition in the category "jerks." I might be allowed these noble thoughts, were I to maintain perfect calm, but I do not. As I note above, I feel a surge to compete, to defend, and to claim what is rightfully mine. Simple as it is in this example, this impulse is the base impulse of power. I want to claim space and privilege over against some other person.

The worst aspect of this whole picture is that I tend to justify my self-assertion in terms of my love of God. Since I, God-fearer that I am, respect laws for the good of my neighbor, then this poor schlep must not honor God. I must risk myself in this encounter (and risk my beloved old Toyota!) in order to try to indirectly remind this person of his or her duty to God and the law. Ha! I am ridiculous, and the height of hypocrisy to boot. This is not love of God or neighbor. It is assertion of power under the guise of love, and it seeks to stake out territory. It is, as we shall see below, love corrupted, for love in its deepest sense becomes love in giving away its power for the sake of the other. The mystery of love, in the Christian tradition, is this: "that love is weaker than selfishness, but therefore is also more creative." Try again: "Love's power *is* its weakness; frail, selfless, surrender to the other is the way it flourishes and thrives." Again: God's love finds its power by "allowing place and recognition to the hostile opposition."

Despite its absolute triviality, somehow ceding space to the assertive drivers willingly, graciously, even to the point of having cars behind me honk, more nearly mirrors the divine love I seek to mirror in the midst of my life. As soon as one moves from the example of the traffic stop to the examples of the history of the Christian church as empire, wielding its faith by the power of the sword in various crusades, or its missionary conquests of the "savages," or even its violent persecution of "heretics," the triviality drops immediately away. It is an awful legacy, given further legitimacy as false use of power by virtue of Pope John Paul II's public apology for them in *Memory and Reconciliation*. The fact is, however, that ever since the Emperor Constantine's embrace of Christianity in the fourth century and his melding of faith and empire, the church has struggled with a legacy of institutional power and its companion, a theology of glory, but always in tension with outbreaks of a revived theology of the cross.

Peter, Jesus's disciple, is a classic example of the tensions of love I've described above. He has a lot of trouble getting past the idea that love is power, and he struggles to understand the meaning—and particular cost—of discipleship. Mark's Gospel records one key moment. As Jesus and the disciples made their way along the road, Jesus asks them what the word is about him. Who, he asks, do people say I am? After hearing such expected responses as John the Baptist, Elijah, or simply a prophet, Peter blurts out his own hope and convic-

145

tion: "You are the Christ, the Messiah" (Mark 8). After telling them to keep this quiet, Jesus then speaks to them about the consequences of this identity as the one God's people had been waiting for to restore the throne of David and free God's people from their suffering under a series of occupations, the latest being imposed by the Romans and their Jewish puppet king, Herod.

Jesus described to them how the Son of Man must suffer, be rejected by the leaders of the day, be killed, and after three days rise again. Peter must have looked at Jesus with his mouth gaping open, for the Bible records that he took Jesus aside and began to rebuke him. Peter, like most of the struggling common people in those days, wanted the Romans and the Jewish leaders to suffer and to see this movement, led by the Messiah, regain the glory of Israel and rule again on the throne in Jerusalem. Jesus's response was uncompromising: "Peter, get out of my way! Satan, get lost! You have no idea how God works" (Mark 8).

Peter must have been dogged by this rebuke for some time, but as the Gospels record the story, he continued to think that love as power might be the way to do God's will as a follower of Jesus. The last dramatic example of this came at Jesus's arrest in the garden near the Mount of Olives. Jesus had gone there after his last supper with the disciples, having shared the bread and cup, and according to John's Gospel, washed their feet to model for them the servant nature of love. Judas, the disciple who betrayed Jesus to the authorities who wanted to arrest Jesus, brought a detachment of Roman soldiers along with a group of police from the chief priests of the temple. Jesus knew they were looking for him, so he stepped forward. But Peter, seizing the moment, drew his sword and attacked, thinking this was the moment to fight and defend the movement they'd been building. He struck at one person and nearly cut off his head. Again, as he did before, Jesus rebukes Peter. "Put back your sword. Do you think for a minute I'm not going to drink this cup the Father gave me?" (John 18).

Jesus did, in fact, drink that cup. It was the cup described by Isaiah in chapter 51 as he called forth the new life from those who had suffered exile, saying "Wake Up! Rub the Sleep from your eyes! Up on your feet, Jerusalem! You've drunk the cup God handed you, the strong drink of his anger." Here, then, are the scriptural roots of Jesus's actions; he is the promised one, the Son of Man, who alone could drink this cup of wrath for us, subverting it in the act of divine self-giving that even in that moment of staggering was already overcoming the inhumanity of those who rejected and killed him.

Peter, it turns out, still had a terrible struggle with Jesus's drinking this cup. He abandons Jesus, effectively denying—three times!—that he ever knew Jesus, and even when he was brought to the empty tomb by Mary Magdalene, "he walked away puzzled, shaking his head" (John 18; Luke 24). It took multiple weeks of time spent with the risen Jesus for Peter to finally understand. This struggle of Peter must reflect the struggle of the early followers of Jesus to make sense of this shocking story—that they might triumph through suffering love rather than love turned toward worldly power. The Gospel of John ends with the capstone of this story of Peter's transformation, and it offers a vision of discipleship that holds to this day.

Having appeared to the disciples on the beach where they were fishing, Jesus arrived when breakfast was on the fire, and so he joined them, breaking bread and fish, sharing it with all of them. When they finished eating, Jesus asked Peter three times, "Do you love me?" Each time, Peter responded, "Yes, Master, you know I love you." And each time Jesus tells Peter "to feed my lambs." Afterwards, Jesus told Peter

I'm telling you the very truth now: when you were young you
dressed yourself and went wherever you wished, but when you
get old you'll have to stretch out your hands while someone
else dresses you and takes you where you do not want to go.

John 21

The author of John, a Gospel written after Peter's death, inserted an editorial comment here: "[Jesus] said this to hint
at the kind of death by which Peter would glorify God." And
indeed, according to the tradition, Peter was martyred under
the Roman Emperor Nero in Rome about AD 64. (I will
return to a discussion of Peter's legacy for the church in the
epilogue.)

St. Paul was the one who most clearly understood and
developed Jesus's teachings on the necessity of his suffering.
He understood the mystery of the Christian faith. He, like
Peter, had to have his wrong-headed understanding turned
upside-down through a dramatic encounter with Jesus. One
piece of this encounter is described in his second letter to
the church at Corinth, chapter 12. There he admitted being
caught up into a vision of heaven, but in order that he not
boast, he was given a thorn in his flesh. He never says what
this thorn was, but he begged the Lord to take it away (here
bringing echoes of Jesus's own prayer that this cup might be
taken from him). Instead, the Lord said to him, "My grace
is enough; it's all you need. My strength comes into its own
in your weakness." This core point helps make sense of all
Paul says in his hymn of love in the first letter to the church
at Corinth: love "isn't always 'me first'" but rather, it "puts
up with anything."

Author C. S. Lewis describe four types of love: affection,
friendship, eros, and charity. The first three, which are entirely
human loves and not divine, are subject to the possibility and

the danger of any human love. They each can become — in the guise of their pure and noble forms — utterly about power and satisfaction of the self. And they can be distractingly powerful even in more mundane ways, as in my example of drivers. In my love for my own power, I lose the divine love in Jesus Christ that alone offers God's own gift of love laid down in weakness, as an abundance that overwhelms the limits of my assertion of power.

The abundance that overwhelms is God's work, but insofar as we live in the love known to us in Jesus Christ, we live laying down our lives in weakness. Martin Luther, commenting on a verse from St. Paul's letter to the Galatians, offers a soaring portrait of this life of love. The passage he was commenting on reads, "For if those who are nothing think they are something, they deceive themselves" (NRSV). Luther comments,

> We are all equal, and we are all nothing. Why, then, does one man puff himself up against another, and why do we not help one another? Furthermore, if there is anything in us, it is not our own; it is a gift of God. But if it is a gift of God, then it is entirely a debt one owns to love, that is to the law of Christ. And if it is a debt owed to love, then I must serve others with it, not myself. Thus my learning is not my own; it belongs to the unlearned and is the debt I owe them. . . . Thus my wisdom belongs to the foolish, my power to the oppressed. Thus my wealth belongs to the poor, my righteousness to the sinners. For these are the forms of God of which we must empty ourselves in order that the forms of a servant may be in us.

Such a patter of self-emptying is what theologian Alan Lewis calls the sublime logic of love. And to remember *this* love and to live it out in our lives is, in the words of U2's song "Walk On," "not the easy thing." We now turn to U2's way of singing love.

Not the Easy Thing

If there is one theme U2 has mined most in search for musical inspiration, it is love. While they can play a down and dirty sexy song with the best of them, what distinguishes U2 is their range of songs drawing on the theme. From bubble-gum affection to erotic desire, from the abiding respect of friendship to the self-giving sacrifice of charity, U2 has explored the range of loves as perhaps no other rock and roll band. Here, multiple song options for each kind of love leap to my mind, and while I'll attempt to stay focused on a small number of key songs, I'll inevitably name-drop some others along the way.

First stop in this tour of love is bubble-gum love, an ode to affection that may lead to casual sex but doesn't fill the deeper need that only a more divine love can fill. "Discothèque" was the lead-off song on the late 1990s album *Pop*. The song is about as fun as U2 gets, and they obviously had fun recording it—they even reportedly put up mirror balls in the studio. Recorded with explicit echoes of the Village People, the song has a pumping beat, and the video features mirror balls, flashing colors, and even the band dressed up camp-style in the uniforms popularized by the Village People. The song's lyrics evoke the pulsing fun of the club scene and the sense of attraction—to the lights, the music, and to the other people dancing.

The song is actually a parable about love, exploring both the fun of pleasure and affection as well as the difference between affection, casual sex, and a deeper yearning not filled through such love. In the fun, then, is also a hidden lament: "You know you're chewing bubble gum / You know what that is but you still want some / You just can't get enough of that lovey-dovey stuff." As is typical, their live versions give the band some space to develop songs, and this one was no different. While the recorded version ends with these lines, I've added in the live additions, taken from a 1998 PopMart tour concert in Mexico City:

> Looking for the one / But you know you're somewhere else instead. / You want to be the song / The song that you hear in your head / Love, love, love. / [You want heaven, heaven, you want heaven in your heart] / But you take what you can get / 'Cause it's all that you can find. / Oh you know there's something more / But tonight, tonight, tonight. / Boom cha, boom cha, discothèque [sound of orgasm]

The "Boom cha" clearly has a meaning beyond the beat of the bass drum. Despite their contrast between a heavenly longing and the very earthly pull of sexual attraction, they are not saying sexuality is in itself bad. Rather, they give sexuality its due as a part of humanity. Later on the *Pop* album they approach the theme of sexual attraction perhaps most memorably in the soulful, searing "If You Wear That Velvet Dress." The erotic can be beautiful but dangerous if it acts as a God-substitute in our lives.

Sex may be fun, it may be dangerous, and it may be shallow, depending on the context, but for sure it is not everything. Love that endures requires something deeper than attraction, however powerful it may seem at the time. Here, U2's catalog includes a series of songs that move toward love as friendship, songs that Bono has written for Alison Stewart, his high school sweetheart and wife of over twenty years. One that has a lovely story behind it is the 1987 song "Sweetest Thing." While it was intended to be a track on that year's hit album, *The Joshua Tree*, it was taken off at the last minute and showed up as a b-side for the single release of "Where the Streets Have No Name." Bono, busy working in the studio ahead of the release of *The Joshua Tree*, apparently worked right through Ali's birthday and wrote the song to try to make it up to her. When the band decided it was too good a song to have languish on a b-side, they rerecorded it for their *Best of the 1980s* album and released it as a single then. It was a number-one hit on the charts.

The video for "Sweetest Thing" features Ali. Although famously camera-shy, she agreed to do it if the proceeds went to support her long-time concern, the Chernobyl Children's Project. The theme of the video is an over-the-top effort on Bono's part to apologize, complete with a horse-drawn carriage, a marching band, and Bono's bandmates serenading the couple. They even pass under numerous street signs that echo a line in the song that says: "I'm sorry for it, really." The sweetest thing, it turns out, is love, and the song is a punchy recognition of the foibles that tear at a long-term relationship and thus need healing. "Blue-eyed boy meets a brown-eyed girl / Oh, the sweetest thing / You can sew it up but you still see the tear / Oh, the sweetest thing."

Some have said that Ali is a saint for putting up with Bono—considering his manic work habits, his penchant for being a disaster groupie, and his long absences from home while touring with the band. Bono has this to say, however, in explaining their longevity:

> I can't remember his quote exactly, but there is a writing by Jean Cocteau where he says friendship is higher than love. Sometimes, it's less glamorous, or less passionate, but it's deeper and kind of wiser, I think. At the heart of my relationship is a great friendship. That's in fact, in many ways, the key to all the important doors in my life: whether it's the band, or whether it's my marriage, or whether it's the community that I still live in. It's almost like the two sorts of sacraments are music and friendship.

Indeed, their love and their marriage has endured because of a deeper love. Temptations of attraction may come, but as Bono sings in a recent love song about his marriage, "I could never take a chance / of losing love to find romance" ("A Man and A Woman" from *How to Dismantle An Atomic Bomb*).

Love that gives itself away—divine love, as C. S. Lewis called it—has been the theme of some of U2's biggest hits. The band's tribute to nonviolence and especially the work of Martin Luther King Jr. did this first and perhaps most powerfully. "Pride (In The Name of Love)" developed, as many songs do for the band, from a sound check before a concert. But musically, the song is rooted in their tour of the Chicago Peace Museum. There, they were deeply moved by the profound story of the American civil rights movement and about the life and leadership of Dr. King. As Edge remembers it, "Because of the situation in our country non-violent struggle was such an inspiring concept. Even so, when Bono told me he wanted to write about King, at first I said, 'Whoa, that's not what we're about.' Then he came in and sang the song and it felt right. It was great."

The song plays off the ways King embodied the self-giving love of Christ. Lines weave back and forth between these two heroes of love: "One man come he to justify / One man to overthrow / In the name of love." Jesus is the one who offers justification "by his grace as a gift" (Romans 3, NRSV). King is the one who struggled to overthrow the system of racism and legal segregation in the American south. Later in the song, another obvious couplet does the same kind of pairing: "One man washed up on an empty beach / One man betrayed with a kiss." King was, so to speak, washed up on an empty beach by the water of the fire hoses white leaders used to stop the civil rights marchers. Jesus's disciple Judas betrayed him by a kiss in the Garden of Gethsemane (Luke 22). And the last verse, all

153

about King, highlights both his murder in Memphis in 1968 and the conclusion of this famous "I Have a Dream" speech given on the Lincoln Memorial during the 1963 March on Washington where he quoted an old spiritual: "Free at last, free at last, thank God Almighty, we're free at last." In "Pride," Bono sings "Early morning, April four / Shot rings out in the Memphis sky. / Free at last, they took your life / They could not take your pride."

During the Rattle and Hum tour in the late 1980s, the band was campaigning for states to ratify the bill to create a new holiday in honor of Martin Luther King Jr. While playing in Arizona, the band got into trouble for this advocacy work and received some death threats. As Bono recalls there was one specific threat, "Don't go ahead with the concert. And, if you do, don't sing 'Pride (In the Name of Love)' because, if you do, I am gonna blow your head off, and you won't be able to stop this from happening." The band decided to go ahead with the concert and to play "Pride." Something dramatic did happen, but not what everyone most feared. Bono, again:

> I do remember actually, in the middle of "Pride," thinking, for a second: "Gosh! What if somebody was organized, or in the rafters of the building, or somebody, here and there, just had a handgun?" I just closed my eyes and I sang this middle verse, with my eyes closed, trying to concentrate and forget about this ugliness and just keep close to the beauty that's suggested in the song. I looked up, at the end of that verse, and Adam was standing in front of me. It was one of those moments where you know what it means to be in a band.

As Jesus said to his disciples, "This is my commandment, that you love one another as I have loved you. No one has greater love than this, to lay down one's life for one's friends" (John 15, NRSV). The deepest mystery of the faith was, on that night in Arizona, both song and band: the power of love *is* its weakness. No, love is not the easy thing. Yet finally it is the only thing that matters.

U2 Songs Embodying Themes of Love

"Into the Heart" (*Boy*); "Two Hearts Beat As One" (*War*); "Pride (In the Name of Love)" (*The Unforgettable Fire*); "With or Without You" (*The Joshua Tree*); "Desire," "Hawkmoon 269," "When Love Comes to Town" (*Rattle and Hum*); "Love Is Blindness" (*Achtung Baby*); "Discothèque" (*Pop*); "Sweetest Thing" (*Best of 1980–1990*); "Walk On" (*All That You Can't Leave Behind*); "Vertigo," "Love and Peace or Else," "A Man and A Woman" (*How to Dismantle an Atomic Bomb*)

Others?

11

Now (Not Yet)

On a personal level, I haven't lost my faith at all. I don't practice it in the same way I did when I was younger, but I haven't lost sight of the fundamentals of it. There are many people out there who would disagree and say, "Well, how can you do this and how can you consider yourself that?"

Larry Mullen Jr.

How Can We Be Saint *and* Sinner?

Christians, despite the advice of their founder, love to throw stones. Not literal ones, mind you, but barbs, pronouncements, and especially eternal judgments. While I was serving as pastor in a church in Connecticut, a couple of men began calling me asking for a meeting. They began attending our weekly Bible study. They listened patiently initially but inserted their agenda slowly and persistently until one day, about a month after meeting them, they confronted me. I was going to hell, it turned out, and leading my flock astray. The culprit? I was willing to say that God would have mercy and offer love and forgiveness to anyone. They desperately wanted to draw up lines with some in and some out. Because I didn't draw lines, I was clearly permissive, liberal, and probably loved sinners. Which was true, at least insofar as I tried to embody God's prodigal love for everyone without regard. But they didn't buy my arguments about the fact that even after being baptized and born again we remain sinful, and thus we can't trust ourselves to judge others—that must be left for God.

As I carefully dissected these arguments publicly and asked that the men leave, I thought I was being patient. But that last day, one older woman who was always one to speak her mind said, "Pastor, I've never seen your angry side before!" And she was right. I was angry, and I took the temptation to throw stones right back at them. I attacked them with cold logic and assertion of my truth over against their truth in some form of power play. While they knew they were being attacked, they stood their ground with me in the hallway, hoping to crack my defenses even in the face of my rising anger. I finally told them if they ever came back I would call the police immediately. Some "love without regard" I was showing.

Imagine my smile when I read of a similar experience for U2. During the tour for the *War* album, when the band was playing "Sunday Bloody Sunday" for the first time in concert, Bono would hoist a long pole with a white flag to make a statement about surrender and nonviolence. Sometimes he would simply run around the stage, other times climb the rafters, and sometimes he would go off into the crowd. One time, Bono recalled, the crowd "wouldn't let me through and I started to fight with the crowd. That big jock had started to block my way, and I lost it in the crush, throwing digs to protect myself,

158

making my statement about pacifism and nonviolence. I don't know what was going on in my head back then."

Philip Yancey describes many prominent Christian leaders who have been excoriated by other Christians for their actions, even when they are as simple and seemingly noble as Eugene Peterson's work with *The Message*, a translation of the Bible into contemporary language. A cult-watch group that accuses him of "tampering with God's word" has targeted Peterson. Hypocrisy, Yancey notes, means "putting on a mask," and Jesus often used the term to describe the Pharisees, a hyper-religious group that seemed to relish in pointing out the faults in other people while claiming to be pure themselves. Yet Jesus critiqued them for dishonesty and said to beware of their influence. Yancey says this is the take-home message from Jesus: "I know of only two alternatives to hypocrisy: perfection and honesty." And since Yancey has never met a perfect human, he argues,

> I do not view perfection as a realistic alternative. Our only option, then, is honesty that leads to repentance. As the Bible shows, God's grace can cover any sin, including murder, infidelity, or betrayal. Yet by definition grace must be received, and hypocrisy disguises our need to receive grace. When the masks fall, hypocrisy is exposed as an elaborate ruse to avoid grace.

The theology of glory has always been tempted to claim perfection. The theology of the cross, however, has developed another way of speaking of life in Christ as being simultaneously saint and sinner. Bono put it in similar terms at one point: "It's funny, but I think there is a real lack of understanding about what we are, the band members and myself. We're all either seen as saint or sinner, when we're all of us—not just the band—a mix of both."

159

St. Paul, writing in his powerful letter to the Romans, spoke of this reality when he lamented, "I decide to do good, but I don't *really* do it; I decide not to do bad, but then I do it anyway." He delights in God's law of love and wishes to follow it, but he finds his arms and legs disobey, that his "flesh" acts differently from what his "spirit" desires. "I've tried everything and nothing helps. I'm at the end of my rope. Is there no one who can do anything for me? Isn't that the real question? The answer, thank God, is that Jesus Christ can and does" (Romans 7). Here, Paul can be misunderstood, and so it is important to be careful. Paul understood there to be two impulses within us: one orienting our whole self toward the world, our self-ish desires, and therefore sin. The other impulse orients our whole self toward God, toward ways to make our lives lives of service to others, and therefore toward grace. This tension within us remains after we are born again; it is a fact of the struggle to live life in Christ.

Since the very early church, Christians have struggled to understand this basic fact present in the life of faith: how is it that once born again through baptism and the holy spirit, sin persists? The key is in the mystery of our justification, our being made righteous, by God for Christ's sake. St. Paul puts it this way in the third chapter of Galatians:

> Until the time when we were mature enough to respond freely in faith to the living God, we were carefully surrounded and protected by the Mosaic law. The law was like those Greek tutors, with which you are familiar, who escort children to school and protect them from danger or distraction, making sure the children will really get to the place they set out for.
>
> But now you have arrived at your destination: By faith in Christ you are in direct relationship with God. Your baptism in Christ was not just washing you up for a fresh start. It also involved dressing you in an adult faith wardrobe—Christ's life,

the fulfillment of God's original promise. In Christ's family there can be no division into Jew and non-Jew, slave and free, male and female. Among us you are all equal.

Humanity was under the judgment of the law. Because of sin people think of themselves with all together too rosy an image, both in their actions toward others and toward God. The law exposes this hypocrisy and calls our prideful, self-inflated self what it is — disobedience to God's law of love (summarized by Jesus as loving God, and loving the neighbor as oneself).

How, then, does faith in Christ offer new life in the face of human sin and evil? Faith in Christ is not some task we humans have to perfect in order to be worthy of God's forgiveness, as if our having enough faith would provoke God's love for us. No, it is the opposite. Christ is both God's favor and God's gift. Christ is God's favor because God's heart is merciful toward us, forgives us, and offers us mercy — the removal of God's wrath. And Christ is God's gift, in that we are really given the presence of Christ to dwell in us and make of us new persons, restored to proper relation to God and to the world. Paul uses baptismal imagery — we are baptized into Christ, that is, die and rise with him, and we are then clothed with him in our new life in Christ. So faith becomes our open hands and open heart with which we receive this favor and gift of God for our salvation.

So we are in one sense wholly sinner and wholly saint: we fall short in our human striving but are clothed with Christ through baptism, making of us holy people before God. This can be said because we in ourselves, in our "flesh" as Paul puts it, are wholly sinners as part of a fallen humanity; we stand guilty (as sinners) before God. Yet because also in ourselves, in our "spirit" as Paul puts it, we have the presence of Christ "in us," we stand as righteous (as saints) before

God. While the wholly sinner, wholly saint perspective is right, it is incomplete without also seeing the partial view that helps explain how we grow in faith and righteousness. Just as Christ defeated evil and death and was raised to new life as a promise of the future fulfillment of all creation, we too receive Christ's presence in faith, but the promise of fulfillment awaits God's time. Thus, because we have received Christ in faith through baptism, we are partly saints, but the "flesh" remains in us and we are tempted by sin, so we also remain partly sinners.

Martin Luther, who is most responsible for this language of the Christian as simultaneously saint and sinner, used the ancient Christian image of Christ as leaven — yeast — in order to explain how this dynamic works in the life of a Christian. In faith we have received Christ into our hearts, as "the leaven hidden in the lump." And like with bread making, "the leaven [is] hidden in the lump; the whole lump has not yet been leavened, but it is beginning to be leavened." As yeast works its way through the whole lump of dough in time, so over our lives Christ "comes to us spiritually without interruption" working in us as the yeast in the dough, filling us with things holy and pure, and putting out of us the things of the "flesh": "greed, lust, anger, pride, terror of death, sadness, fear, hate." This is like U2 in their song "Yahweh" where Bono sings, "take this mouth / so quick to criticize / take this mouth / give it a kiss." God's kiss covers a sharp tongue. In biblical terms, we truly have Christ present with us in faith, but where sin remains Christ covers us; we are counted a saint on his account. Living this contradiction, this paradox, in faith means that all does not have to be resolved. As Martin Luther said to a friend, "if grace is true, you must bear a true and not a fictitious sin. God does not save people who are only fictitious sinners. Be a sinner and sin boldly, but believe and rejoice in

Christ even more boldly, for he is victorious over sin, death, and the world."

Cockeyed Idealists

While Bono is the spokesperson for U2 in many ways, on the issue of living the contradictions of a life of faith, the Edge has a central voice. He was the one who went away for two weeks alone to ponder the conflict between faith and rock music that almost broke up the band before they got started. And it was his painful divorce that underlies the contradiction and confusion that showed up in force on the 1990 album *Achtung Baby* and in some ways underlined that whole decade of U2's work.

When journalist Bill Flanagan asked the Edge about U2's early struggles, and how he, Larry, and Bono had doubts about being Christians and being in a band, Edge responded, "It was reconciling two things that seemed for us at that moment to be mutually exclusive." Recalling that time, the Edge said: "We were getting a lot of people in our ear saying: 'This is impossible, you guys are Christians, you can't be in a band. It's a contradiction and you have to go one way or the other.'" So he took some time for reflection and came back to tell the band his decision: "Okay, it's a contradiction for some, but it's a contradiction that I'm able to live with. I just decided that I was going to live with it. I wasn't going to explain it because I can't." Not surprisingly, the experience soured the band on a certain form of Christianity famous for claiming to have resolved contradiction and for throwing stones at those on the other side of clarity. Comparing then to now, Edge says, "The central spirit of the band is the same. But I have less and less time for legalism now. I just see that you live a life of faith. It's nothing to do necessarily with what clothes you wear or whether you drink or smoke or who you're seeing or not seeing."

Ironically, U2 had its own season of throwing stones during the 1980s. Bono describes it as a humorless period when they took on issues they cared about, trying to change the world through rock and roll. They became more and more famous as the decade went on, but as critical press grew, they became more self-conscious about being perceived as both critical of success and power while becoming successful and powerful themselves. In critiquing the televangelists with the line "preachers stealing hearts in a traveling show" (in the song "Desire"), Bono began to realize that he himself was a preacher stealing hearts in a traveling show. Such realizations led him to "decide the only way was, instead of running away from contradictions, I should run into them and wrap my arms around them and give 'em a big kiss. Actually write about hypocrisy."

The album *Achtung Baby* allowed singing contradictions to fully come into flower. Edge described the themes of the album as "Betrayal, love, morality, spirituality, and faith." Interestingly, I haven't dealt with the topic of betrayal so far, and all the three songs that came to me for this chapter are from *Achtung Baby*, perhaps most deeply influenced by Edge's divorce and the themes of betrayal, contradiction, and paradox. The journey is painful, in part because the members of U2 take commitment so seriously. As Bono describes it, "It all gets back to the fact that it's an extraordinary thing to see two people holding on to each other and trying to work things out. I'm still in awe of the idea of two people against the world, and I actually believe it is to be against the world, because I don't think the world is about sticking together." Whereas in the past, U2 had written about the contradictions out in the world, now they found themselves in the midst of them and decided that being right in the middle of a contradiction was "the place to be." The band still holds high ideals, but now they are not surprised by the pain and difficulty and compromise in living their faith. As Bono said recently, "Please, please, please! Don't ever see me as a sort of wide-eyed idealist who only sees the good in people. Cockeyed, maybe."

Perhaps the classic song of U2 as cockeyed idealists is the vulnerable track titled "Acrobat" on *Achtung Baby*. In what could be a bittersweet love song, instead U2 gives a driving introduction with bass pushing and drums pounding, and growling guitar reminiscent of "Bullet the Blue Sky." Bono remembers the context of *Achtung Baby* and "Acrobat" particularly:

> Well, as you get older, your idea of good guys and bad guys changes. As we moved from the eighties to the nineties, I stopped throwing rocks at the obvious symbols of power and the abuse of it. I started throwing rocks at my own hypocrisy. That's a part of what that work was about: owning up to one's ego. These characters in the songs like "The Fly" are owning up to one's hypocrisy in your heart, your duplicitous nature. There's a song called "Acrobat" that goes: "Don't believe what you hear, don't believe what you see / If you just close your eyes you can feel the enemy."

The sense of confusion and the discovery of internal conflict becomes stronger as the song goes on. A poignancy enters as Bono sings, "And I'd join the movement / If there was one I could believe in / Yeah, I'd break bread and wine / If there was a church I could receive in. / And I must be an acrobat / To talk like this and act like that." Opening honestly to this place of contradiction allowed their work to expand its creativity, taking alternative points of view in order to see more deeply into the crevices of life's pain and joy.

Two songs enter exactly into places of pain and joy, exploring relationships between friends where expectations are high, and yet we let one another down profoundly. While neither "Until The End of the World" nor "One" is directly about marriage, betrayal is a theme central to both. The first is U2's treatment of the great betrayal: that of Judas betraying Jesus. Written for a film by their friend, the German director Wim Wenders, the song fits with the band's long-standing fascination with sin and apostasy. Songs on 1987's *The Joshua Tree*, such as "Exit," a dark song about a psychotic killer, or "Running to Stand Still," about a heroin addict, are clear early examples of Bono seeking to understand something he's not experienced personally. In an interview, he suggests that some U2 songs are like overheard conversations. "They're not my stories, but I feel them very deeply." So it is with "Until the End of the World." The song describes the tensions in the relationship between Jesus and Judas from the perspective of Judas. The lyric portrays Jesus and Judas as very close and recalls the last night they were together. Its rough, jarring beat combines with a jabbing guitar, but Bono, as Judas, sings in a low voice, as if recollecting a time long ago when, "We were as close together as bride and groom, / we ate the food, we drank the wine / everyone having a good time except you / You were talking about the end of the world."

Judas recalls taking the money from the Romans, paid so that he would betray Jesus to the soldiers at the right time. And indeed, the night before he died, Jesus was in the garden on the Mount of Olives praying when Judas came with a cohort of soldiers and other religious leaders. The agreed-upon sign, a greeting with a kiss, led to this line: "In the garden I was playing the tart / I kissed your lips and broke your heart." But soon Judas regretted his betrayal, and the song ends with a vision of, even here in the heart of darkness and sorrow, God's ability to make even this wrong right. Bono, as Judas, sings these last lines to end the song, "Waves of regret and waves of joy. / I reached out for the one I tried to destroy / You, you said you'd wait till the end of the world." While on the Elevation tour in 2001, the Edge portrayed Jesus and Bono portrayed Judas, and they each walked out the ellipse on opposite sides of the half circle toward each other, meeting in a climactic guitar solo where Bono/Judas falls down but reaches up toward Edge/Jesus, screaming. The heart of contradiction: reaching out for the one you have betrayed.

"One," the song just prior on the album, portrays a similar feeling of betrayal and reaching out for healing despite the hurt. Considered by many as U2's finest song, "One" came out of the initial efforts to "dream it all up again," as Bono famously promised at their New Year's Eve concert at the Point Depot in Dublin, 1989. They envisioned going to Berlin as the wall was falling, looking for the fresh enthusiasm of freedom there to inspire them. Instead, they found a depressingly dirty city, awful weather, and recording studios in terrible condition. On top of that, they were not on the same page at all musically, with Edge and Bono pushing a radical redirection and Adam and Larry arguing for a more modest shift. Worst of all, they were not getting any new ideas that actually pulled together into a song. While they have always jammed together as a means of inspiring new songs, with Bono singing nonsense (what he calls "Bonoese") along with the music, now they were months into their efforts with nothing to show. Tempers were growing short.

Then, in a flash, while working on a chord for what became "Mysterious Ways," they hit a groove and Bono began improvising at the mike, "Is it getting better, or do you feel the same? / Will it make it easier on you, now you got someone to blame?" They had, in a matter of minutes, taken down the bones of the song. It is a swaying ballad, as U2 does so well, and its lyric goes right into the heart of pain. "You say one love, one life, when it's one need in the night. / One love, we get to share it / Leaves you baby if you don't care for it." The bitterness comes out—thinking of their recent fights in the band, and the underlying tensions with Edge's breakup: "Love is a temple, love the higher law / You ask me to enter, but then you make me crawl / And I can't be holding on to what you got, when all you got is hurt." Yet in the midst of the despair, they cry out nonetheless for a way toward healing. "One love, one blood, one life, you got to do what you should / One life with each other: sisters, brothers / One life, but we're not the same / We get to carry each other, carry each other." Like many U2 songs, "One" has had lives beyond its origin. Written out of a place of pain and contradiction, when it was released as a single it was designated for an AIDS benefit. Its theme of unity and carrying each other despite pain became a powerful vehicle for the release of emotion—from their long-awaited concert in Sarajevo in 1997 where the crowd carried the hoarse-voiced Bono to the incredibly touching version from the PopMart tour in Mexico City that the band dedicated to the memory of a close friend, Michael Hutchence of INXS, who had just committed suicide. "One" became the backdrop during the Elevation tour in 2001 when they projected the names of the people who were killed on September 11. More recently it became the rallying call for the "One" campaign during the Vertigo tour, with the band inviting concert-goers to text message their names to sign up for the campaign.

In some respects, their openness to the movement of the Spirit makes the embrace of paradox necessary. They never could have guessed the way a song that was born in betrayal and frustration would become such a cry for hope and strength in adversity. Yet U2 sees how they are part of something much

168

bigger, something that they contribute to but does not come from them. Their embrace of the fact that, despite their short-comings, they know that the gift of God's blessing and mercy lives in them heals more, touches more, and inspires more than they could ever hope to do on their own. It is, in a way, the biggest contradiction of all that a rock and roll band understands itself as wrapped up in a conspiracy with the God of heaven and earth. Yet that's U2. Larry: "If we thought it was all about us, it would f**k us up. Something happens, but it is not something we make happen. It only happens when God walks through the room."

U2 Songs Embodying Themes of Saint and Sinner

"I Fall Down" (*October*); "Drowning Man" (*War*); "Bad" (*The Unforgettable Fire*); "Exit" (*The Joshua Tree*); "God Part II (*Rattle and Hum*); "One," "Until the End of the World," "The Fly," "Acrobat" (*Achtung Baby*); "Yaweh" (*How to Dismantle an Atomic Bomb*)

Others?

STEP THREE . . .

12

SINGING THE TRUTH

Never trust a performer, performers are the best liars.
They lie for a living. You're an actor, in a certain sense.
But a writer is not a liar. There's a piece of Scripture:
"Know the truth, and the truth will set you free." Even
as a child, I remember sitting, listening to my teacher in
school talking about the great Irish poet William Butler
Yeats. He had writer's block—there was a period where
he couldn't write. I put my hand up and said: "Why didn't
he write about that?"—"Don't be stupid. Put your hand
down. Don't be so cheeky." But I didn't mean it as a
smart-arse. I have lived off that idea: Know the truth, the
truth will set you free.

Bono

Thus far, I have offered an analysis of U2's music as a religious
icon, as a "spiritual pointer finger" urging others to look under
the trash of late modern life for the element of soul. They urge
their audience on in seeking this picture of life—but it is not

about some generic spiritual seeking. After all, in the song "Mofo" from their 1997 album *Pop*, it was "the baby Jesus" they were looking for under the trash. U2's studio and live work as a band is, as I've tried to show, deeply resonant with a scriptural and theological tradition the church has called "theology of the cross," a worldly and doubtful interpretation of the Christian faith that seeks above all to speak the truth about humanity, the world, and God.

The first part of the book showed how the band draws on a rich palette of scripture to paint the vivid colors of the truth about our lives. In the second part I showed the resonances between the band's songs and performance and the theology of the cross, set against its rival, the theology of glory, by the use of simple pairings: faith, not sight; hope, not possession; and love, not power. The interpretive work thus far means to show biblically and theologically how U2 seeks to "sing the truth." It now remains to sum up just what I mean, and what I think U2 means, by "truth," and why such an interpretation of Christianity is so needed today. I will do this in a more general way here, describing its scriptural roots, then I'll briefly say something about how the band exemplifies living the truth in this way. Finally, in the epilogue I'll offer a summary vision that orients those seeking God to a spiritual model faithful to the discipleship of the cross embodied in the work of U2.

The Truth that Frees

I came to this study of U2 convinced that they stared down the path of truth—even if it meant admitting doubt, even if it meant crying out against violence and longing for peace and justice, even if it meant feeling impotent in the face of worldly power. Bono describes it as a sort of insatiable curiosity that leads him to pick up the rocks of life and look at the creepy-crawlies living underneath. I implicitly knew this through their songs. Anyone paying close attention knows they've gone to the secret places where fear and desire and hate reside in their hearts, and mine, too. I was drawn deeply into their music, their lyrics, and their lives because of the authenticity I found there. And the deeper I've gone into their thought, writing, music, and lives, the more clear it is to me that this point is key. Bono says as much in the quote above, and there are many occasions where similar sentiments are offered regarding the importance of truth.

The key question to ask, however, is the question that Pilate, the Roman governor, asks Jesus during his trial: "What is truth?" (John 18). Jesus does not answer Pilate, but he had ample opportunity to explain his views on truth prior to that climactic moment. Bono, especially, has said how meaningful John's Gospel is to his understanding of truth. That is the source of the quote he refers to above, "Know the truth and the truth will set you free." It bears looking into in order to shed light on how this understanding of truth makes sense of U2, their music, and their lives. In the Gospel of John, this passage comes at the end of a section taking place during a Jewish festival, and the clear overtone is that of conflict and danger.

At the start of this section, in John chapter 7, Jesus is only moving about quietly in his home region of Galilee because the leaders are looking "for a chance to kill him." His brothers challenge him to go to Judea (the region to the south of Galilee that includes Jerusalem) to make a public display of the works he was performing. Jesus declines, saying, "This isn't my time." His brothers go, and Jesus follows later in secret. The leaders are looking for him at the festival, and people are talking about him, debating if he is good or if he is a deceiver. Nonetheless, Jesus couldn't keep quiet. Halfway through the festival, he went up to the temple area and began to preach. In order to discredit Jesus, they claimed he had no teacher. Here, in his response, Jesus gives a first clue about the meaning of truth.

Jesus first claims that his teaching is not his own, but it comes from God. And he challenges the people listening by saying that if they chose to live according to God's teaching, they would know that Jesus speaks of God and not on his own. Jesus then makes this key distinction: "A person making things up tries to make himself look good. But someone trying to honor the one who sent him sticks to the facts and doesn't tamper with reality." After some back and forth, equally pointed, "many in the crowd committed themselves in faith to him" and "the Pharisees, alarmed at this seditious undertow going through the crowd, teamed up with the high priests and sent their police to arrest him." Jesus keeps on preaching, however, and even the temple police were convinced (they said, in their own defense when they showed up back at the temple HQ without having nabbed their man, "We've never heard anyone speak like this man").

Yet the leaders judge him guilty as a dangerous rebel, and they are frustrated by their failure to arrest Jesus. So it is highly significant that the next section, just leading up to the key quote about truth, is about not passing judgment. First, in John 8, the scribes and Pharisees bring forward a woman caught in adultery, saying that she ought to be stoned according to the law of Moses and asking for Jesus's opinion, hoping to trap him with the question. Instead of responding right away, Jesus bent down and wrote in the dust with his finger. The scribes and Pharisees continued to pester Jesus until finally he looked up and said, "The sinless one among you, go first: Throw the stone." And he bent down, taking up his drawing in the dust. Jesus stood up, asking the woman if indeed no one had condemned her. Standing completely alone, having watched her would-be accusers depart, she said, "no one." And Jesus replied, "Neither do I. Go on your way. From now on, don't sin."

In the next section, where Jesus speaks of his light as a gift to his followers as they walk in darkness, he declares to his hearers, "You decide according to what you can see and touch. I don't make judgments like that." Yet his very identity passes cosmic judgment on sin and darkness, and so he continues, "But even if I did, my judgment would be true because I wouldn't make it out of the narrowness of my experience but in the largeness of the One who sent me, the Father." This judgment is not about good or bad actions but about fundamental alienation from God—the alienation that Jesus came to overcome. These passages are more or less parallel, then, but in reverse:

1. "If you won't believe I am who I say I am, you're at the dead end of sins."
2. "If you stick with this, living out what I tell you, you are my disciples for sure. Then you will experience for yourselves the truth, and the truth will free you."

In the first, Jesus describes the danger of missing the truth of his presence in their midst as the incarnate word, God's very presence (drawing on God's name as revealed in Exodus 3, NRSV—"Say to the Israelites, 'I AM has sent me to you'"—and here the deeper meaning of the U2 song, "All Because of You," which continues in the very next line, "I AM" [*How to Dismantle an Atomic Bomb*]). In the second, Jesus describes how one can embrace the truth of his presence: because he comes to abide in us, and as we receive that gift, we know the truth (I AM), and the truth sets us free.

It is almost as if the freedom comes from being captive to God's word. If we abide in the word, that is, if we — in faith — welcome Jesus to abide in us, then we are free. Free from the slavery of "sin" as the woman caught in adultery was set free. Free from fear of punishment, free from suffering and death, and full of the light of God that shines in the darkness. Free because Jesus has stared into the worst of human evil in his own rejection and death on the cross, and by God's faithful promise he arose on the third day.

This mystery, this promise, is bound to us in faith as we welcome Jesus to abide in us (John 15). As a result, we no longer need to fear the dark, no longer fear death, nor any evil. It is the freedom to speak truthfully about the world and to face the consequences. It is, in fact, the liberation of the soul — not for heaven, but for abundant living here on the earth. The liberation of the soul allows us to really dig into the life of the world and to give ourselves away in love. It is this liberation of the soul that Jesus brought to the wedding at Cana where, when the wine ran out, he turned water into wine. It is this liberation of the soul that led Jesus to break religious rules by speaking to the woman at the well (John 4), healing on the Sabbath (John 5), asking to have dinner at the home of Zacchaeus (Luke 19), or angrily overturning the tables of the money changers in the temple court (John 2). It was this liberation of the soul that made Jesus love the world so much that he drank the cup of suffering, rejection, and death rather than run away or pick up weapons to fight. It was this liberation of the soul that Jesus spoke of when he said, "know the truth, and the truth will set you free." Living this truth is, then, living discipleship to Jesus and his way of the cross.

Some people may have thrown this book across the room after reading these last paragraphs about living the truth as a way of following Jesus. If you have done that and are now picking the book up to see where things go next, let me assure you I *do* see the irony in saying that super-rich rock stars who live a charmed life, who smoke, drink, and swear, are living "the way of the cross." Let me say something direct about this "walking the talk" issue as I close out the chapter.

The Art of the Possible

There is a thread of people throughout history who have lived the theology of the cross and who, despite struggling in grave times and great personal suffering, found strength to live the truth of their faith. They knew, each of them, about the way of the cross as the way to life. Why? Because in trusting the truth of that way, the way of the cross, they no longer feared death and could be free to give themselves away in love as each of them had the opportunity. It turns out that, as an example, Martin Luther King Jr. wrote powerfully about his life and struggles, and this bearing of his soul in speeches and books is one means by which he gave himself to the world. But he and many others gave their witness in their place and time because they felt they could not do otherwise. They felt their lives had, in a sense, been taken and blessed and broken and poured out, and their gift and task was to give themselves over to the ways God was using them for the sake the world.

U2 has this self-understanding as well. From the passionate spiritual truth-seeking and intense desire to see justice done for the poor, to the Flannery O'Connor-like overdrawn and hilarious portrayal of images of sin and grace and persistence in staring evil in the face with love, U2 has deep resonances with the lives lived in this way of the cross. In an interview, Bono struggles to articulate what this means to their music:

179

If you're true, if you describe what's in your life, or in the room, or what you pick up—because of a lot of our songs, I feel like they're overheard conversations. Sometimes they're not my stories, but I feel them very deeply. But to be true is really important, and that seems to get you truth. God is interested in truth, and only in truth.

Great music, like great lives, moves us to see with more clarity the things that really matter in life. As I move to the last section of this chapter, I will venture some thoughts on how U2 lives the truth. I don't want to pry past what is public about the band, and at the same time I feel that part of the power of U2 is that their music and lives go hand in hand. They are, in their lives, pointing to a way in the world, and it is a way that can be described as the way of the cross.

As they've grown as a band it has become clearer (though it has always been part of the band's ethos) that singing the truth is not enough; they have to live it. One can trace this conviction from the early letter Bono wrote to this father stating that U2 would become "more than a great band" to his recent admission that "U2 is about the impossible. Politics is the art of the possible. They're very different, and I'm resigned to that now." While this section is not simply about politics in the traditional sense, it is about how the members of U2 structure their lives together, and that in one sense is the heart of politics. In order to do this with organization, I'll move through what might be called spheres of life, commenting in each one on ways U2 as a band and its members individually live the "art of the possible."

To begin with, it makes sense to discuss their art. They make their instruments sing—drums, bass, guitar, piano, harmonica, voice, and more. They were not originally strong musicians and have clearly improved in this area—they understood that they were handicapped in this respect, and so they have worked hard as a result. During times off from recording and touring, various members of the band have taken lessons to improve their skills. And they have befriended many talented musicians who have lifted the quality of their craft. The Edge, who had considered medicine and has the mind of a scientist, has delved into the technical side of music production, and the whole band has grown in their use of technology as an aid to their music.

They also, as a band, embrace poetry in the writing of songs. They depend on Bono to write most of the songs, but Edge, as well as Adam and Larry, add ideas to varying degrees. For the first few albums, Bono tended to let the music lead, improvising lyrics at the mike as the Spirit moved him. The band has always had the feeling—not unlike Flannery O'Connor in her writing—that revelation will come if they wait and pay attention. Bono especially, but the whole band to some extent, began to read poets and songwriters from various genres for inspiration. The effect of this reading especially took hold with *The Unforgettable Fire* and its opening song, "A Sort of Homecoming" that by any account shows lyric inspiration and carries echoes of the German-Romanian poet Paul Celan and the great Irish poet William Butler Yeats. Producers have had their say, as well, from Brian Eno playing American gospel records to Howie B playing techno and retro vibes to inspire the band. The band has continued to grow in their poetic and lyric skill, not only learning the conventions of songwriting but becoming masters at the art.

They have also developed a taste for drama, but in truth it was something that predated U2. Bono often talks about a performance group he formed with his friends in their teenage years. Called the Lypton Village or just the Village, the group of friends put on avant-garde art shows and dressed in punk and glam outfits that sent his father into a huff. While their early live concerts tended to be more light and sound shows, with their ZooTV tour in the early 1990s, U2 has developed the most innovative shows in the business. It was on ZooTV that Bono began to experiment with various alter egos, from the Fly with his oversized shades to Mr. McPhisto and his devil horns. Bono in fact credits this move from their "humorless" period in the 1980s to the drama, irony, and humor that played out in the 1990s to his reconnection to friends from Lypton Village. Still, despite their ability to work with show designer Willie Williams and many other talented artists to put on visually interesting shows and produce creative videos for singles, Bono still holds up his end of a long-standing debate with a Village friend, Guggi. Bono argues that art is about ideas. Guggi, refusing to give in, says "No, art is about paint." In the end, U2's performance art is in the tension between these views and the strong people in U2's world who argue for them at every juncture.

The art of relationships has also been central all along the way. Family has its obvious connections in song lyrics—from early songs on *Boy* and *October* about Bono's mother to the touching tribute to his father on their latest album, from songs evoking the pain of Edge's divorce on *Achtung Baby* to the powerful story of a "Miracle Drug" that gave their childhood friend, Christopher Nolan, the ability to communicate. And the band itself has been family for the four members, given especially that both Larry and Bono lost mothers at an early age. It is almost unheard of for a band to remain together for almost thirty years, despite troubles and tensions of various sorts. The song "One" is a classic example of the healing fruit of tension in the band; as the lyric goes, "we're one, but we're not the same / we get to carry each other."

They have, over time, integrated their own growing families into the life of the band. They've all maintained homes in

Dublin. And remarkably, the band maintains local friendships they've had since their early days. When they are away from home, they are often together. Edge and Bono own condos next to one another in the south of France where they spend part of the year. Their children (all but Adam have kids) show up at concerts and even on stage at various points on tour. Humorously, the Edge found it nerve-wracking to hear his own teenage daughter and her friends review *How to Dismantle an Atomic Bomb*. These relationships—to friends, family, and community—speak to a conscious effort to overcome the vertigo of being rock stars so that they can find ways to be normal people.

Even though the band avoids rock star hubris with family and friends, they've always tried to use their rock star fame for political purposes. They decided very early on that they would transgress the rule that rock bands don't sing about religion and politics. They went beyond that to aggressively use their fame to promote ideas they believed in, beginning with their effort to portray a position of Christian nonviolence in response to the "troubles" in Northern Ireland embodied in their famous anthem, "Sunday Bloody Sunday." It is no surprise, then, that in their most recent tour, they combine their new song "Love and Peace or Else" with "Sunday Bloody Sunday" to comment on the current world tensions between the three faiths of Father Abraham: Islam, Judaism, and Christianity.

Their politics is not simply in their singing, however. They hold fast to an unusual democratic politics within their band's structure, splitting revenue and decision making equally between the four band members and their manager, Paul McGuiness (although increasingly McGuiness is out on artistic decisions). While the various contributions of the band members ebb and flow, their commitment to making financial and artistic decisions together has been unwavering. They have on principle turned down millions of dollars in endorsements in order to not have their songs used in commercials. They gave Apple Computer permission to use their single "Vertigo" as an act of support for a company they like very much, and for significant public relations gain for their new single (it hit number one and won a Grammy, and gained U2 a new generation of digital music listeners who put "Vertigo" on their iPods). It was an agreement of mutual appreciation, done without any payment in either direction.

Their albums (and their website, U2.com) include information on supporting various political causes the band feels strongly about, including Greenpeace, Amnesty International, War Child, Jubilee 2000, and the Chernobyl Children's Project (Bono's wife, Alison, has worked on this project for more than ten years). They have also supported many, many more local funds and charities. They helped to found DATA (Debt, AIDS, Trade, Africa), an organization that focuses on support for positive social change in Africa. They campaigned for a national holiday for Martin Luther King Jr. in the U.S., against apartheid (they were the first band invited to come to the newly free South Africa), against the violence in the former Yugoslavia (their broadcast of live footage of the bombing of Sarajevo during the ZooTV tour raised awareness, and they were the first band to play in Sarajevo after the cease-fire was achieved), and against various kinds of dictatorships and political violence (in Chile, El Salvador, Burma, and more). The proceeds from the number one single "The Sweetest Thing," because it was written by Bono for Ali, were all donated to her long-term concern, the Chernobyl Children's Project (and it was U2's biggest selling single ever).

As in this last example of the donation of proceeds from a U2 single to charity, the band is clear that politics connects directly to economics. They have been as active on that front as with strictly political causes. They wrote a song about a tough mining strike in Britain in 1984 called "Red Hill Mining Town" and recorded a powerful economic interpretation of "Jesus Christ" written by folk legend Woody Guthrie. That song, recorded in Sun City Studios in Memphis where Elvis recorded, included such lines as, "Well Jesus was a man / Who traveled through the land / A hard working man and brave / Well he said to the rich 'Give your money to the poor' / For they laid Jesus Christ in his grave / Hale, hallelujah." Even if the members of U2 are rich, none of them grew up rich, and they have given back to those in need.

One very admirable and often overlooked fact of U2's organization is their business loyalty. They have, from early on, made a commitment to Dublin. Their homes, recording studios, and management offices are all in Dublin, and they have brought development to Dublin because of it. Together, the band bought and refurbished a classic old downtown hotel, the Clarence, and they have been faithful to a host of people who work with and for them, including (for example) their sound engineer Joe O'Herlihy, who has been with them every tour for over twenty years. While they have fun and enjoy their personal success, they have been attentive to the fact that their success gives work to an increasing number of people who work for their organization in Dublin and beyond.

On a more international level, the band has passed around the wealth by giving away proceeds from concerts, singles, charity items, and sections of their tours. In the summer 2005 run up to the Live 8 concerts, planned by Sir Bob Geldof to raise awareness for the campaign to "make poverty history," the band announced that each of the members plus manager Paul McGuiness would donate one million euro (a gift totaling more than six million U.S. dollars) from the 2005 Vertigo tour to support the campaign. Prior to this, the band has participated in Live Aid, which led to the summer Bono and Ali spent in Ethiopia. Afterwards, Bono and the band backed an ever-evolving set of activities related to Africa, including the very prominent Jubilee 2000 effort aimed at releasing the crushing debt of the poorest nations. Their Live 8 concert tied to the "One" Campaign sought to influence the so-called "Group of 8" wealthy nations to double international development aid to the poorest nations in an effort to eliminate extreme poverty by the year 2025.

To make the point that debt relief and development aid is only one part of the equation, Bono and Ali have worked with the fashion designer Rogun to create a high-end "fair trade" fashion line called Edun ("nude," spelled backwards, and evoking the purity of the biblical garden of Eden). The company is based on "four respects"—respect for where the clothes are made, for those who make them, for the materials, and for the consumer who buys them.

If all that I've said thus far is true, then it makes some sense to say that U2 lives their faith, living the truth that their lives are not their own but belong to others. At the end of their very personal and provocative *How To Dismantle an Atomic Bomb* book (sold with the CD in a deluxe edition), a book that begins with death and ends with life, they write "We wish these truths were self evident but . . . we need a new declaration of interdependence to remind ourselves . . . that men and women were created equal and in serving each other we discover the meaning of our lives." Those who try to live in the manner of Christ, following the way of the cross, might be expected to also be close to the church. This, however, is not a simple equation. U2 has never had an easy relationship with the institutional church.

This is, in part, the fate of all those who really grasp the theology of the cross and its call to follow with humility and in solidarity with the world. Flannery O'Connor spoke of a blind and deaf age, an age that needed her violent and dramatic presentation of the gospel to make space for the repentance and transformation at the heart of the faith. Martin Luther King Jr. struggled relentlessly with churches (both white and black) that resisted change and did not admit his claims for justice, leading him to say the church was most alive on its margins and not in the church pews.

And it is so for U2. They have been critical of a church that has been too soft-spoken on issues of justice and has been too loudly critical of U2. For more than a thousand years (since Constantine, the Roman emperor, converted and declared Christianity the faith of the empire) the Christian church has lived in a convenient but ultimately deadly marriage to the powers of this world. And it is U2's confrontation with power and wealth in their push for greater aid for Africa's poorest who are dying from preventable causes at an alarming rate (some estimates are one every three seconds) that has raised the band's strongest words for the church. Touring the heartland of the United States during winter 2002–2003, Bono said:

> There should be civil disobedience on this. You read about the apostles being persecuted because they were out there taking on the powers that be. Jesus said, "I came to bring a sword." In fact, it's a load of sissies running around with their "bless me" clubs. And there's a war going on between good and evil. And millions of children and millions of lives are being lost to greed, to bureaucracy, and to a church that's been asleep. And it sends me out of my mind with anger.

Despite suggesting that most churches are "a bunch of sissies running around with their 'bless me' clubs," the purpose of the trip was not condemnation. Bono was seeking to change hearts and minds. He stepped into pulpit after pulpit in Midwestern churches, meeting with the famous and the infamous in an effort to share what in his mind was entirely compelling logic: "It's absolutely clear what's on God's mind. You just have to read Scripture. Those who read Scripture and don't come away with God's preferential concern for the poor are just blind given that there are 2,103 verses of Scripture about the poor."

But U2's ambivalence about traditional Christianity has roots in their experience growing up in a land torn apart by factions defined by religion. The Protestant-Catholic divide cast a long shadow over "religion" in Ireland in a complicated set of ways, and not only in terms of political power (the Church of Ireland, a Protestant church tied to the Anglican Communion, is the church of the upper class, as well). So when Bono wonders aloud if "religion is the enemy of God" and suggests that "religion is what happens when the Spirit has left the building," the roots of such sentiments are fairly understandable! U2's formative religious experience as a band comes out of the distinctly nondenominational, Spirit-filled atmosphere at their Catholic-Protestant union high school, Mount Pleasant. Larry, Edge, and Bono, along with others, were deeply shaped by the intense community in the Shalom Fellowship where they lived communally and studied the scriptures in depth. Bono recalls that, "We got a great grounding in the fundamentals of what Christianity could be. It wasn't particularly Catholic or Protestant, it was more the cutting edge of Christianity. And I'm really glad we have that base."

As I've made clear throughout the book thus far, their music is alive with their faith convictions. Many fans, and the band itself at times, refer to U2 concerts as "going to church." Bono: "Music is the language of the Spirit anyway. Its first function is to praise creation—to praise the beauty of the woman lying next to you or the woman you would like to lie next to you."

Speaking of U2's 2001 Elevation tour, Bono said, "It feels like there's a blessing on the band right now. People are saying they're feeling shivers—well, the band is as well. And I don't know what it is, but it feels like God walking through the room, and it feels like a blessing, and in the end, music is a kind of sacrament." Many Christians like to pick on the band for their lack of participation in church, citing such lyrics as "Acrobat," where Bono sings, "I'd break bread and wine / if there was a church I could receive in." Actually, from the perspective of the cross, the reverse is true. The church ought to be asking itself what it is that keeps U2 and their millions of God-hungry fans on the edges of the church rather than coming inside and finding the abundant life Jesus promises.

So much of the church's energy goes into its own self-perpetuation (check a budget sometime), its buildings, clergy, and trappings of holiness. What if instead the church was known, as Jesus wanted, by its love? I'll leave you with these words from the song "Mercy," which was left off *How to Dismantle an Atomic Bomb* but will likely be on their next album:

> Love believes me when I lie / Love puts the blue back in my eye / Love is the end of history / the enemy of misery / Love refuses to believe that equality / is just for the naïve / Love has got to be for the weak / Only then does love get a chance to speak.

Despite all their worldly trappings of wealth and power, in U2 love does get a chance to speak. And we who seek to follow on the way, seeking to be disciples and to be faithful, can find through U2 a means to have love speak in us, through us, for the world.

189

Epilogue

. . . To Knowing

I was talking to Noel Gallagher [from the band Oasis]
about my dad, who lost his faith toward the end of his life.
And Noel asked, "Does he believe in God?" And I said, "I
don't think he knows." So Noel went, "Well, he's one step
closer to knowing now." And I thought, "I'm going to write
that song . . ."

Bono, describing the origins of the song "One Step Closer"

I hope some of the people who read this book don't know
very much about faith and aren't sure about God. I hope
some of those people read to this point and are thinking:
"Maybe I want to try out that way of life, even if I haven't
always been turned on by what I've seen in church or from
other Christians." But perhaps you've been a Christian for a
while, or, like me, grew up in the church and have become
fed up with churches that too often seem uncomfortably like
what Bono describes as "bless me clubs." If that is you, then
this book is for you.

191

I've described an understanding of the Christian life that has deep roots in the tradition, is faithful to Jesus, and fits U2. I've called it the theology of the cross, and I've offered it here as a way of seeking God. It is not an understanding of the faith that lets us climb a ladder to God. It is a faith that, by recognizing that God came to us, lived with us, died for us, and now lives in us by his Spirit, frees us to really live in and for the world.

My friend and colleague Miroslav Volf calls this view of the Christian life "soft difference." This view of the Christian life helps summarize what I've described in this book, and so now I'd like to use it as a simple way to describe this way of living the truth, of following Jesus, in and for the world. And in doing so, I'll be clearer about why U2 "gets a lot of stick" for their faith both from the rock and roll side and from the faith side. To set up what Volf has to say, I'll first describe these two sides—the rock and roll side and the faith side—showing the perspectives they come from in critiquing U2.

On the one hand, some voices say that the band's faith should make no difference in their music and public life. I'm referring to critics who say, "Oh, please, get off your high horse and be a proper rock and roll band." These critics—including fellow rockers and many music fans and writers—get tired of U2 and especially Bono pontificating about this or that cause. They claim the band has sold out for corporate rock, and any support for a cause starts a lot of eye rolling from those who have grown tired of the high-profile star-with-a-cause activism. Many people of faith who cut against the grain have been told to shut up as well, and the band has struggled long and hard with its "hearts on their sleeves" approach. Even when they turned to much more humorous and ironic presentation of their ideas in the 1990s, it was only heart in another guise.

192

On the other hand, other voices say that the band's faith should make a stronger difference in their music and public life. The classic critique, mentioned earlier in the book, regards the band's anthem of faith and doubt titled "I still Haven't Found What I'm Looking For." Why, if their faith is sincere, can't U2 simply proclaim in unequivocal terms that Jesus is the answer and they have found what they're looking for? Such critics bemoan that U2 has received awards from "wicked MTV" and has at various points indulged in strong drink, smoking, and cursing. This perspective argues, "The world loves U2 because U2 is of the world." For anyone who knows the Bible, this is a slam that draws on Jesus's famous admonition to his followers to be "in, but not of, the world."

No difference, or a hard difference that builds a wall between the believer and the world. Are these the options? If they are, I'm not a follower of Jesus either. I want something else, something that admits my doubts and failings while freeing me to embrace the world for the sake of witnessing to the abundant life possible in God. In a long article reflecting on the biblical book of 1 Peter, Miroslav Volf talks about the community to whom this letter was written nearly two thousand years ago. Prior to conversion, these Christians were surrounded by people they considered neighbors. After becoming Christ's disciples, they found they didn't fit quite as well in former routines. They became, as the text says, "aliens" in their own city.

This alien identity is, Volf says, "a bursting out of the new precisely with the proper space of the old." Our lives, while remaining in the midst of the world, are made new. This new life, given in baptism, can take two forms as it works itself out in relation to the old world. One is a negative process of rejecting the beliefs and practices of others. The other option entails a positive process of giving allegiance to something distinctive. Given that they were a minority group under some suspicion, the community 1 Peter describes does not argue for wholesale revolution against the norms of the surrounding culture. Rather, they are to be the change they wish to see in the world, a perspective that has echoes from Jesus through Gandhi to U2. "To make a difference, one must be different," Volf writes.

The author of 1 Peter withholds power as a means to force a change in the world. Rather, the means (soft difference, and not hard) is through meekness, gentleness, and fearlessness. The last of these is key. Fear drives assimilation or rejection: become like me or get away from me. Soft difference makes a way for people to live without fear, and "mission fundamentally takes the form of witness and invitation. They seek to win others without pressure or manipulation, sometimes even 'without a word' (1 Peter 3:1)." But soft difference is not simply a missionary method; it is "following in the foot steps of a crucified Messiah. It is not an optional extra, but part and parcel of Christian identity itself."

Such an approach is deeply needed today. It is not simply a means in our individual journeys to take one step closer to God. It is, in the face of hatred and terror, a way forward given to us from the crucified Messiah. This way offers Christians a path in the world that is faithful to God's way in the world. God, the love and logic of the universe, became human as a baby in order to live and suffer and ultimately save the world. That means that the way of weakness and humility, of love and suffering, of giving our lives to and for the world, is already blessed. U2 has found that way to follow Jesus. They point us toward it. And this book serves its purpose if one or two find their way one step closer to knowing this way.

NOTES

Introduction

9   "somebody following you: it's God.": Jon Pareles, *New York Times*, section 2, page 29, column 2 (November 14, 2004).

10   "if U2's members and music are sufficiently 'Christian.'": "Bono's Thin Ecclesiology," *Christianity Today* (March 2003), 37; Steve Stockman, *Walk On: The Spiritual Journey of U2* (Orlando: Relevant Books, 2001), 2ff.

10   "grown up without any connection to the church.": George Barna, "The Barna Update: One In Three Adults Is Unchurched" available at www.barna.org.

11   "the meaning of U2 songs": See Niall Stokes, *U2 Into The Heart: The Stories Behind Every Song* (New York: Thunder's Mouth Press, 1996, 2003, 2005).

11   "spiritual journey from *Boy* to *How to Dismantle an Atomic Bomb*.": See Stockman, *Walk On.*

11   "investigation of the private life of Bono": See Mick Wall, *Bono: Saint and Sinner* (New York: Thunder's Mouth Press, 2005).

11   "an effort either to defend U2's faith": See esp. Stockman, *Walk On.*

11   "preaching to spiritually hungry but religiously disaffected young people.": See Raewynn J. Whiteley and Beth Maynard, *Get Up Off Your Knees: Preaching the U2 Catalog* (Cambridge, MA: Cowley Publications, 2003).

11   "God will lay a special blessing on you": This kind of theology is and has been prominent in many successful TV preachers over the last thirty years. For a contemporary version of blessings theology, see Joel Olsteen, *Your Best Life Now: 7 Steps to Living at Your Full Potential* (New York: Warner Faith, 2005).

11   "cookies and coffee to the pop music and practical, uplifting messages": See Jonathan Mahler, "The Soul of the New Exurb," *New York Times Magazine* (March 27, 2005); the church is Radiant in Surprise, AZ (www.radiant.com).

12   "calls a thing what it really is.": Martin Luther, "The Heidleberg Disputation," in *Martin Luther's Basic Theological Writings*, ed. Timothy F. Lull (Minneapolis: Fortress Press, 1989), 44.

17 "style of talking about selfhood.": Rowan Williams, *Lost Icons: Notes on Cultural Bereavement* (New York: Continuum, 2003), 7.

Chapter One: Singing Scripture

23 "*Song of Solomon*, the book of *John*": Bono, "Introduction to the Psalms" in *Psalms, Grove Press Edition, With an Introduction by Bono.* (New York: Grove Press, 1999), ix.

25 "a force of love and logic behind the universe.": Bono, quoted in Cathleen Falsani, "Bono's American Prayer," *Christianity Today* (March 2003), 39.

25 "Jesus's acts of feeding": All four Gospels in the New Testament record a story about Jesus feeding a group of people with a few loaves and fishes. See John 6:1–59.

26 "there for people who aren't.": Bill Flanagan, *U2 at the End of the World* (New York: Bantam Doubleday, 1995), 480.

26 "yourself out there into the world.": From an interview with Ann Powers, *Spin*, (March 1997), quoted in Henry Vanderspek, *Faith, Hope, and U2: The Spirit of Love in U2's Music* (Toronto: Dare Connexions, 2000), 7.

27 "rather than through rational explanations.": Ellen F. Davis, *Proverbs, Ecclesiastes, and the Song of Songs* (Louisville: Westminster John Knox Press, 2000), 2.

Chapter Two: Psalms

29 "or 'Answer me when I call' (Psalm 5).": Bono, "Introduction to the Psalms" in *Psalms, Grove Press Edition, With an Introduction by Bono* (New York: Grove Press, 1999), viii.

33 "a cry against violence.": Niall Stokes, *U2 Into The Heart: The Stories Behind Every U2 Song* (New York: Thunder's Mouth Press, 2003), 38.

34 "there's a piece of that in there.": Robert Hilburn, "The Songwriters-U2-Where Craft Ends and Spirit Begins," *Los Angeles Times* (August 8, 2004), available in archive on www.@U2.com.

36 "a cry of desperation and abandonment.": Brian Walsh, "Wake Up Dead Man: Singing the Psalms of Lament," in Raewynne J. Whiteley and Beth Maynard, *Get Up Off Your Knees: Preaching the U2 Catalog* (Cambridge, MA: Cowley Publishing, 2003), 39.

38 "I want to align my life with that.": Cathleen Falsani, "Bono's American Prayer" *Christianity Today* (March 2003), 39.

39 "Christ the only helper.": Dietrich Bonhoeffer, *Psalms: The Prayer Book of the Bible* (Minneapolis: Augsburg, 1974), 49.

Chapter Three: Wisdom

43 "And it's only one book!": Bill Flanagan, *U2 at the End of the World* (New York: Bantam Doubleday, 1995), 434.

45 "the more of God, the less of the human." Eugene Peterson, "Introduction to Wisdom," *The Message* (Colorado Springs: NavPress, 2002), 837

45 "and respond to him believingly": Ibid.

49 "no ordinary assurances could satisfy." Ellen F. Davis, *Proverbs, Ecclesiastes, and the Song of Songs* (Louisville: Westminster John Knox Press, 2000), 163.

51 "a woman rising from a tomb.": Oscar Wilde, "Salomé," in *The Portable Oscar Wilde*, ed. by Richard Aldington and Stanley Weintraub (New York: Penguin Books, 1981), 393.

51 "standard throughout the ZooTV tour.": Flanagan, *U2 at the End of the World*, 63.

52 "the spirit is a feminine thing.": Niall Stokes, *U2 Into The Heart: The Stories Behind Every U2 Song* (New York: Thunder's Mouth Press, 2003), 104.

53 "than any established religion credits.": Anthony DeCurtis, "The Beliefnet Interview," (February 2001), available at www.beliefnet.com/story/67/story_6758_1.html.

54 "novelist whose writings are favorites of the band.": Bono said about Flannery O'Connor in an interview with the band's fan magazine, *Propaganda*, "I've never felt such sympathy with a writer in America before." Ian Gittins, ed., *U2: The Best of Propaganda* (New York: Thunder's Mouth Press, 2003), 63.

55 "you draw large and startling figures.": Flannery O'Connor, "The Fiction Writer and His Country," in *Collected Works of Flannery O'Connor* (New York: Library of America, 1988), 805–6; See also Jill Peláez Baumgaertner, *Flannery O'Conner: A Proper Scaring, Second Edition* (Chicago: Cornerstone Press, 1999).

Chapter Four: Prophecy

57 "fall asleep in the comfort of our freedom.": Ian Gittins, ed., *U2: The Best of Propaganda* (New York: Thunder's Mouth Press, 2003), 67.

58 "bless-me clubs": Bono, quoted in Cathleen Falsani, "Bono's American Prayer," *Christianity Today* (March 2003), 40.

59 "evoking an alternative order.": Walter Brueggemann, *The Prophetic Imagination* (Philadelphia: Fortress Press, 1978), 62.

63 "U2 writes songs and goes on tour, singing them.": Eugene Peterson, "Introduction," in Raewynne J. Whiteley and Beth Maynard, *Get Up Off Your Knees: Preaching the U2 Catalog* (Cambridge, MA: Cowley Publishing, 2003), xii.

63 "sincere egomania": Jon Pareles, "When Self-Importance Interferes With the Music," *New York Times* (October 16, 1988).

63 "go away and dream it all up again": Bill Flanagan, *U2 at the End of the World* (New York: Bantam Doubleday, 1995), 4.

64 "he will tell you the truth.": Ibid., 6.

65 "but you sold me religion.": Beth Maynard, www.u2sermons.blogspot.com.

66 "we're trying to recreate the feeling of sensory overload": Niall Stokes, *U2 Into The Heart: The Stories Behind Every U2 Song* (New York: Thunder's Mouth Press, 2003), 114.

66 "Jean Baudrillard": In his classic work, *Simulacra and Simulation*, Baudrillard begins with a version of a quote from Ecclesiastes, "The simulacrum is never what hides the truth—it is truth that hides the fact that there is none. The simulacrum is true." (Ann Arbor: University of Michigan Press, 1995), 1.

66 "C. S. Lewis": When a fan climbed on stage to question Bono while dressed up as MacPhisto during a ZooTV tour concert, Bono said, "Did you ever read *The Screwtape Letters*? That's what this is." C. S. Lewis, *The Screwtape Letters* (San Francisco: HarperSanFrancisco, 2001).

66 "to describe the age and challenge it.": Flanagan, *U2 at the End of the World*, 66.

67 "the sort of brown-rice position.": Ibid., 477.

67 "careful. And smart.": Ibid., 22.

67 "has been unfairly ignored.": Stokes, *U2 Into The Heart*, 39.

68 "It's very disturbing.": Ibid., 40.

68 "to have to live with that possibility.": Ibid., 40.

69 "already contributed to a turnaround in thinking.": Ibid., 72.

69 "called Glide Memorial.": Flanagan, *U2 at the End of the World*, 100.

70 "in the song 'Bullet the Blue Sky.'": Michka Assayas, *Bono in Conversation with Michka Assayas* (New York: Riverhead Books, 2005), 182.

71 "This will never happen again!": Flanagan, *U2 at the End of the World*, 266.

71 "has that in its backbone.": Stokes, *U2 Into The Heart*, 147

71 "working on the Jubilee 2000 campaign.": See the story in chapter one of Noreena Hertz, *The Debt Threat* (New York: HarperBusiness, 2004).

72 "absurd power he could employ for good.": Steve Stockman, *Walk On: The Spiritual Journey of U2* (Orlando: Relevant Books, 2001),169–170.

72 "100 billion dollars.": Assayas, *Bono in Conversation*, 88.

Chapter Five: Parables

75 "idly curious who 'having ears, do not hear . . .'": John Smith, "The New U2," *On Being* (November 1, 1993) found on www.@u2.com.

76 "clues to what that intention might have been.": John Dominic Crossan, *The Dark Interval: Towards a Theology of Story* (Allen, TX: Argus Communications, 1975), 93–95.

77 "turn, and find forgiveness.": Ched Myers, *Binding The Strong Man: A Political Reading of Mark's Story of Jesus* (Maryknoll, NY: Orbis, 1988), 171.

80 "the most spiritually centered of the band.": Michka Assayas, *Bono in Conversation with Michka Assayas* (New York: Riverhead Books, 2005), 64.

80 "God needs the advertising.": Assayas, *Bono in Conversation*, 147.

82 "a moment a lot of people feel.": Niall Stokes, *U2 Into The Heart: The Stories Behind Every U2 Song* (New York: Thunder's Mouth Press, 2003), 120.

82 "works at that hospice.": Bono, quoted in "The Bomb Squad: U2's Track by Track Guide to How To Dismantle An Atomic Bomb," *Q* (October 2, 2004); see also news archive at www.@U2.com.

83 "the advantage of these things": Assayas, *Bono in Conversation*, 148.

83 "parable of the rich man and Lazarus from Luke's Gospel.": I learned much from the interpretation of Steven Miyamoto posted on the forum on Songmeanings.com.

85 "that moment I started this journey.": Speech by Bono to Britain's Labour Party Conference, September 29, 2004, Brighton, UK (see text at www.data.org/archives/000605.php).

85 "I don't even know what that says about us.": Bono, Labour Party Speech.

86 "that street goes round the world.": Assayas, *Bono in Conversation*, 197.

Chapter Six: Apocalypse

89 "rock 'n' roll is very powerful.": Bono in *U2 Magazine* 10 (1984), 3.

89 "anyone in the audience.": Bono, Interview with Erik Philbrook, *Playback* (December 4, 2001), available in archive at www.@U2.com.

90 "victimized by some form of deprivation.": Paul D. Hanson, "Apocalypses and Apocalypticism: Introductory Overview," *Anchor Bible Dictionary* (New York: Doubleday, 1992), 1:280.

96 "as it is in Heaven.": Michka Assayas, *Bono in Conversation with Michka Assayas* (New York: Riverhead Books, 2005), 203.

97 "some of its ails and its evils.": Assayas, *Bono in Conversation*, 122.

99 "where the streets have no name . . .": Ian Gittins, ed., *U2: The Best of Propaganda* (New York: Thunder's Mouth Press, 2003) 77.

102 "And I can finally make sense of it.": Greg Kot, "Bono: We Need To Talk," *Chicago Tribune* (May 22, 2005), available in archive at www.@U2.com.

Chapter Seven: Singing the Cross

107 "through the gates of heaven.": Michka Assayas, *Bono in Conversation with Michka Assayas* (New York: Riverhead Books, 2005), 204.

108 "what it actually is.": Martin Luther, "The Heidleberg Disputation," in *Martin Luther's Basic Theological Writings*, ed. Timothy F. Lull (Minneapolis: Fortress Press, 1989), 44.

109 "'because, therefore' proposition.": Eric W. Gritsch and Robert W. Jenson, *Lutheranism: The Theological Movement and Its Confessional Writings* (Philadelphia: Fortress Press, 1976), 42–44.

110 "the best-selling book *The Prayer of Jabez*": Bruce Wilkinson, *The Prayer of Jabez: Breaking Through to the Blessed Life* (Sisters, OR: Multnomah, 2000).

110 "but it was never much loved.": Jürgen Moltmann, *The Crucified God: The Cross of Christ as the Foundation and Criticism of Christian Theology*, trans. R.A. Wilson and John Bowden (Philadelphia: Fortress Press, 1974), 3.

111 "best in our religion.": Gerhard Forde, *On Being a Theologian of the Cross: Reflections on Luther's Heidelberg Disputation* (Grand Rapids: Eerdmans, 1997), 2.

111 "the middle of human existence.": Robert Kolb, "Luther on the Theology of the Cross," *Lutheran Quarterly* XVI (2002), 7.

111 "patch up life to please God.": Ibid., 8.

112 "our Christian selves.": Douglas John Hall, "The Theology of the Cross for Our Day," *Lutheran* (March 2004), 14.

113 "the most secular of saints.": Josh Tryangiel, "Bono's Mission: The World's Biggest Rock Star is also Africa's Biggest Advocate," *Time* (February 23, 2002), available in archive at www.@U2.com.

113 "'E's just a very naughty boy!'": Assayas, *Bono in Conversation*, 148.

114 "illusionary self-deification" Jürgen Moltmann, *The Crucified God*, 69.

115 "throwing people off that trail.": Bono, televised interview, transcribed from the video. Website address: http://www.lasvegassun.com/sun/dossier/events/u2/video.html.

115 "that about wraps us up!": Lisa Robinson, "U2's Unforgettable Fire," *Vanity Fair* (October 25, 2004), available in archives at www.@U2.com/archives.

Chapter Eight: Faith

117 "make sure you can trust it.": Ian Gittins, ed., *U2: The Best of Propaganda* (New York: Thunder's Mouth Press, 2003), 226.

120 "Only the suffering God can help.": Dietrich Bonhoeffer, *Letters and Papers from Prison, The Enlarged Edition*, translated by Reginald Fuller, Frank Clarke, et al. (New York: MacMillan, 1972), 361.

120 "Suffering is in God.": Jürgen Moltmann, "The Crucified God," *Theology Today* 31, 18.

121 "the genius of this.": Michka Assayas, *Bono in Conversation with Michka Assayas* (New York: Riverhead Books, 2005), 125.

122 "about the band: our faith.": Ibid., 24.

122 "and testing their temptations,": Bill Flanagan, *U2 at the End of the World* (New York: Bantam Doubleday, 492.

123 "there it is: the same yearning.": Assayas, *Bono in Conversation*, 25.

123 "what is underneath is not so sweet." Gittins, *U2: The Best of Propaganda*, 228.

123 "you can still hear the hissing.": Ibid., 228–29.

124 "both precious and trashy.": Niall Stokes, *U2 Into The Heart: The Stories Behind Every U2 Song* (New York: Thunder's Mouth Press, 2003), 128.

124 "techno carnival.": Ibid.

125 "an anthem of doubt more than faith.": Ibid., 65.

125 "Squeakers": Flanagan, *U2 at the End of the World*, 434.

127 "doing a combination version.": Transcribed from *Rattle and Hum* (DVD version) Paramount Pictures, 1999.

127 "Wow, what an experience!": Bono, transcribed from an audio clip posted on BBC Radio 2, http://www.bbc.co.uk/radio2/soldonsong/songlibrary/istillhaventfound .shtml.

Chapter Nine: Hope

129 "It's really powerful.": Anthony DeCurtis, "The Beliefnet Interview," February 2001, available at www.beliefnet.com/story/67/story_6758_1.html.

130 "official optimism.": Douglas John Hall, *Lighten Our Darkness: Towards an Indigenous Theology of the Cross* (Philadelphia: Westminster Press, 1976), 43.

130 "faith in God's grace and providence.": Douglas John Hall, "Beyond the Cross of Calvary," *Lutheran* (March 2004), 17.

131 "sinners, who arrested Jesus.": Philip Yancey, *What's So Amazing About Grace?* (Grand Rapids: Zondervan, 1997), 274.

132 "say, 'Can you work with me?'": *HM* (March-April 2002), available in archive at www.@U2.com.

132 "and how God loves.": Yancey, *What's So Amazing About Grace?*, 53.

132 "was lost has been found.": Henri J. M. Nouwen, *The Return of the Prodigal Son* (New York: Doubleday Image), 114.

133 "Shouldn't divine love be beyond wrath?": Miroslav Volf, *Free of Charge: Giving and Forgiving in a Culture Stripped of Grace* (Grand Rapids: Zondervan, 2006).

134 "hope for overcoming the strife.": Jürgen Moltmann, *The Crucified God: The Cross of Christ as the Foundation and Criticism of Christian Theology*, trans. R.A. Wilson and John Bowden (Philadelphia: Fortress Press, 1974), 185.

135 "tore off a corner of the darkness.": Ian Gittins, ed., *U2: The Best of Propaganda* (New York: Thunder's Mouth Press, 2003), 67.

136 "light for walking through darkness.": See Garth Beavon's note on "Ultraviolet (Light My Way)" at http://hem.bredband.net/steverud/U2MoL/AB/violet.html.

137 "just try to make the light brighter.": Michka Assayas, *Bono in Conversation with Michka Assayas* (New York: Riverhead Books, 2005), 85.

138 "sermons drawing on U2 lyrics.": Derek Walmsley, "Finding The Way to the Playboy Mansion," Raewynne J. Whiteley and Beth Maynard, *Get Up Off Your Knees: Preaching the U2 Catalog* (Cambridge, MA: Cowley Publications, 2003), 95.

140 "through the gates of heaven.": Assayas, *Bono in Conversation*, 204.

140 "Bono's favorite hymn.": Ibid., 129.

141 "poorer neighborhoods of the city.": See www.DATA.org.

141 "take to keep them alive.": Martin Wroe, "Tears are not Enough" *Express* (December 2, 2002), available in archive at www.@U2.com.

141 "atrocious mathematics.": Yancey, *What's So Amazing About Grace?*, 59.

142 "a part of something like that.": Gittins, *U2: The Best of Propaganda*, 67.

Chapter Ten: Love

143 "Now, that's not so easy.": Michka Assayas, *Bono in Conversation with Michka Assayas* (New York: Riverhead Books, 2005), 200.

145 "recognition to the hostile opposition.": Alan Lewis, *Between Cross and Resurrection: A Theology of Holy Saturday* (Grand Rapids: Eerdmans, 2003), 253.

145 "John Paul II's public apology for them": John Paul II, *Memory and Reconciliation: The Church and the Faults of the Past* (December 1999), available at www .vatican.va.

148 "affection, friendship, eros, and charity.": C. S. Lewis, *The Four Loves* (New York: Harcourt, Brace, 1960).

149 "forms of a servant may be in us.": Martin Luther, *Lectures on Galatians, 1519, Luther's Works*, Volume 27, translated and edited by Jaroslav Pelikan (St. Louis: Concordia Publishing, 1963), 393.

152 "sacraments are music and friendship.": Assayas, *Bono in Conversation*, 119.

153 "and it felt right. It was great.": *Q Magazine* (December 1998) available in archive at www.@U2.com.

154 "thank God Almighty, we're free at last.": James Melvin Washington Jr., ed., *A Testament of Hope: The Essential Writings of Martin Luther King, Jr.* (San Francisco: HarperCollins, 1986), 220.

154 "able to stop this from happening.": Assayas, *Bono in Conversation*, 121–22

154 "means to be in a band.": Ibid.

Chapter Eleven: Now (Not Yet)

157 "you consider yourself that?": Bill Flanagan, *U2 at the End of the World* (New York: Bantam Doubleday, 1995), 488.

158 "that must be left for God.": Jessica Leavenworth, "Prophets of Doom Challenge Area Clergy," *Hartford Courant* (February 15, 2003), available at www.courant .com.

201

159 "in my head back then.": Michka Assayas, *Bono in Conversation with Michka Assayas* (New York: Riverhead Books, 2005), 213.

159 "tampering with God's word": Philip Yancey, *What's So Amazing About Grace?* (Grand Rapids: Zondervan, 1997), 202.

159 "putting on a mask": Ibid.

159 "alternatives to hypocrisy: perfection and honesty.": Ibid., 203.

159 "an elaborate ruse to avoid grace.": Ibid., 204.

159 "a mix of both.": "I Still Haven't Found What I'm Looking For," *Hot Press Magazine* (December 1, 1988), in archives at www.@U2.com.

161 "God's favor and God's gift.": Tuomo Mannermaa, *Christ Present in Faith: Luther's View of Justification* (Minneapolis: Fortress Press, 2005), 57.

162 "the leaven hidden in the lump.": Martin Luther, *Lectures on Galatians, 1535, Luther's Works*, Volume 26, trans. and ed. Jaroslav Pelikan (St. Louis: Concordia, 1963), 350.

162 "it is beginning to be leavened.": Ibid.

162 "terror of death, sadness, fear, hate.": Ibid., 350–51.

163 "over sin, death, and the world.": Martin Luther, *Luther's Works*, Volume 48, trans. Gottfried G. Krodel (Philadelphia: Fortress Press, 1963), 283.

163 "moment to be mutually exclusive.": Flanagan, *U2 at the End of the World*, 47.

163 "to go one way or the other.": Ibid.

163 "explain it because I can't.": Ibid., 48.

164 "who you're seeing or not seeing.": Ibid., 49.

164 "Actually write about hypocrisy.": Ibid., 57.

164 "spirituality, and faith.": Ibid., 82.

164 "is about sticking together.": Ibid.

165 "the place to be.": Ibid., 83.

165 "only sees the good in people. Cockeyed, maybe.": Assayas, *Bono in Conversation*, 85.

165 "you can feel the enemy.": Ibid., 95.

166 "I feel them very deeply." "Bono: A Conversation: A New York Times Event at the Graduate Center of the City University of New York" (March 16, 2003), transcribed from audio available at www.nytimes.com/ref/arts/music/20030417talks-bono.html.

167 "Tempers were growing short.": Flanagan, in *U2 at the End of the World*, gives a great interpretation of this time. See chapter one, "Brezhnev's Bed."

169 "when God walks through the room.": David Fricke, "U2 Dissect 'BOMB,' " *Rolling Stone* (December, 2004), available in archive at www.@U2.com.

Chapter Twelve: Singing the Truth

173 "the truth will set you free.": Michka Assayas, *Bono in Conversation with Michka Assayas* (New York: Riverhead Books, 2005), 36.

180 "and only in truth.": "Bono: A Conversation: A New York Times Event at the Graduate Center of the City University of New York" (March 16, 2003), transcribed from audio available at www.nytimes.com/ref/arts/music/20030417talks-bono.html.

180 "more than a great band": Bill Flanagan, *U2 at the End of the World* (New York: Bantam Doubleday, 1995), 524.

180 "I'm resigned to that now.": Josh Tryangiel, "Bono's Mission: The World's Biggest Rock Star is also Africa's Biggest Advocate," *Time* (February 23, 2002), available in archive at www.@U2.com.

182 "No, art is about paint.": Flanagan, *U2 at the End of the World*, 153.

187 "out of my mind with anger.": Cathleen Falsani, "Bono's American Prayer," *Christianity Today* (March 2003), 43.

188 "2,103 verses of Scripture about the poor.": Ibid.

188 "the Spirit has left the building": Anthony DeCurtis, "Bono: The Beliefnet Interview" (February 2001), www.beliefnet.com/story/67/story_6758_1.html.

188 "glad we have that base.": Joe Jackson, "Bono Vs. The Beast: A Guided Tour Through U2's New Album," *Musician* (August 1, 1993), available in archive at www.@U2.com.

188 "you would like to lie next to you.": DeCurtis, "Beliefnet Interview."

189 "music is a kind of sacrament.": Chris Heath, "U2 Tour: From the Heart," *Rolling Stone* (May 10, 2001), available in the archive at www.@U2.com.

189 "love does get a chance to speak.": U2, *How to Dismantle an Atomic Bomb, Deluxe Edition Book* (New York: Universal, 2004), 23.

Epilogue: . . . To Knowing

191 "I'm going to write that song . . .": "It Could Be About God," *Blender* (October 17, 2004), available in archive at www.@U2.com.

192 "soft difference.": Miroslav Volf, "Soft Difference: Theological Reflections on the Relation between Church and Culture in 1 Peter," *Ex Auditu*, http://northpark.edu/sem/exauditu/papers/volf.html.

192 "gets a lot of stick": Joe Jackson, "Bono Vs. The Beast: A Guided Tour Through U2's New Album," *Musician* (August 1, 1993), available in archive at www.@U2.com.

193 "The world loves U2 because U2 is of the world.": For this critique, see the Way of Life Ministries, www.wayoflifeministries.org/fbns/rockgroupu2.html.

193 "the proper space of the old.": Volf, "Soft Difference."

194 "To make a difference, one must be different.": Ibid.

194 "part and parcel of Christian identity itself.": Ibid.

ACKNOWLEDGMENTS

I wrote this book primarily for young people—those in high school and college. Others might find it, read it, and find it speaks to them. If so, I will be gratified.

Yet this book is for the high school youth like those in my confirmation classes at First Lutheran Church of the Reformation, New Britain, Connecticut, who pulled me into theological reflection on pop music. I remember the Christmas vividly when I used a Coolio song in my sermon—to the delight of the youth and the horror of their parents. I did it because the youth thought Coolio came up with the lyric, "As I walk through the valley of the shadow of death" and were shocked to find he was actually quoting the twenty-third Psalm. Thanks, all of you, for teaching me how to be a teacher for you.

The book is for college students like those in the Lutheran Student Movement of New England, a combination of the Lutheran campus ministry groups throughout the New England states. They asked me to lead a retreat on the theme, "grace in the wilderness—the theology of the cross and its contemporary relevance." I quickly made plans to use this retreat to explore the idea that the theology of the cross fit with U2's way of speaking of God and the world. I searched on the web for "grace in the wilderness" and a week later had Eoghan Heaslip's praise and worship CD from CORE, an inner city church in Dublin Ireland. Ha! Only much later did I find out Eoghan's father, Jack, was a counselor at Mt. Pleasant High School where U2 began, and after becoming a Church of Ireland priest, served as an unofficial chaplain for the band. Unfortunately, the retreat was canceled and I never got to present the material in retreat form. So of course, I had to write a book!

Rodney Clapp is responsible for the book coming out as a Brazos title. After a session on worship and ethics at the Society for Christian Ethics, we struck up a conversation and he asked what else I was working on. His eyes lit up when I mentioned this project, and I happily sent him a prospectus. A few weeks later, I had a contract and the book was underway. At every point Rodney and Rebecca Cooper, managing editor at Brazos, have been encouraging and helpful in shepherding the book along toward publication.

Too many people write books and don't say where or how. Thanks to Starbucks in New Haven on Chapel and High and their high-energy barristas. Many chapters were hammered out there. And thanks to Apple for my iBook (that has not crashed once since I bought it and happily keeps my digital box set of U2's music readily at hand).

I want to thank Eugene Peterson though I've never met him. His energetic portrayals of the beauty, seriousness, and spirituality of the pastoral life inspire so many of us who care about the integrity of ministry and the church. And that commitment motivated his production of *The Message*, a translation of the bible in such vibrant language that it simply jumps off the page. U2 loves the translation, but that is not the only reason I used it here. I love it, too, and Peterson wrote it for just the sort of seeker audience U2 plays for and I've written for. One quibble: God is not a man, and Father is only one of many biblical terms used to call upon the Holy One of

Israel. Yet *The Message* usually uses male pronouns for the first person of the Trinity. For the integrity of the translation, I've left quotes as they are, but it bothers me and I know it will bother some of my readers. U2's way of calling out to God using the personal pronoun "you" avoids all the trouble.

My profound thanks U2—Bono, Edge, Adam, and Larry—and their organization. The whole book is a thank you letter for your role in giving expression to so much that I feel and pressing me to live life awake, seeking truth and justice, and trusting grace through it all. Thanks also to the U2 fandom online, especially Beth Maynard at U2sermons, Angela Pancella and Matt McGee at @U2, as well as many others who leave comments on Songmeanings, Interference, U2Tours, and the list goes on. U2 fans are a pretty insightful bunch, and undoubtedly I'll become the subject of their debates as this book sees the light of day.

Thanks to Steve Stockman, Bill Flanagan, and, later on, Michka Assayas for writing important and thoughtful books about U2. The only source I quote more often is the Holy Bible!

Some friends and mentors directed me on the path that led to this book. First of all, Timothy Lull and Don Saliers taught me theology and modeled theological reflection on pop music. Douglas John Hall taught me to read Luther's theology of the cross in today's context and to write critically for our contemporary culture. David Miller and Miroslav Volf, my friends and colleagues at the Yale Center for Faith & Culture, provided vibrant intellectual and material support. Our administrative assistant, Lucinda Gall, who loves opera and choral music, happily learned to listen to U2 in the office over the last few months and helped in many other ways as well. Thanks to Chris Jones and Kathryn Reklis, both theology graduate students at Yale, who read the manuscript at various points and saved me from many mistakes. For those that remain, I apologize.

Finally, Sonja, thank you for your engagement with and excitement about this project. Thanks for our home and life together. Thanks for sharing faith and life commitments and for the amazing partnership in parenting we share. I dedicate the book to our children, Isaiah (age 7) and Grace (age 5). As they grow, may this book serve as a way to share with you, to paraphrase 1 Peter 3, "why we're living the way we are." I will always laugh thinking of you dancing around the house singing, "El-le-va-tion." I also dedicate the book to Rose, our sponsor child in Malawi, whom we hope to meet someday and who focuses our prayers and interconnections with the work of justice and love that transcend every boundary. Where she lives should not decide whether she has adequate food, medicine, and education.

May the words of my mouth and the meditations of my heart be acceptable in Your sight, my rock and my redeemer. Amen.

New Haven, CT
October 26, 2005

Commemoration of Philipp Nicolai, Hymnwriter (1608)

"Wake, awake, for night is flying.
The watchers on the heights are crying.
Awake, Jerusalem, at last."

Save the Children
54 Wilton Road
Westport, CT 06880
www.savethechildren.org

DATA
1400 Eye Street, NW, Suite 1125
Washington, D.C. 20005
www.data.org